A LETTER TO T

Dear Disciple,

The Bible assures us in Jeremiah 29:11 that God has a wonderful plan for our lives, to give us a future and a hope. I pray that the Lord will use this discipleship workbook to help you grow in your understanding of the truths contained in each lesson, and that you will gain a deeper intimacy with Jesus Christ.

Jesus commissioned the church to make disciples,

> *"Go therefore and make disciples of all the nations, baptizing them in the name of the Father and the Son and the Holy Spirit, teaching them to observe all that I commanded you; and lo, I am with you always, even to the end of the age."*
> Matthew 28:19-20

A disciple is a student or a learner, one who walks so closely with his master that he becomes like him in his thinking and behavior. In Matthew 10:25, Jesus told His disciples, *"It is enough for the disciple that he become like his teacher..."* We become like our Master and Teacher, Jesus Christ, by spending time alone with Him, talking to Him in prayer and listening to Him speak to us in His Word.

In John 15:4, Jesus said, *"Abide in Me, and I in you. As the branch cannot bear fruit of itself unless it abides in the vine, so neither can you unless you abide in Me."* To abide means to have intimacy and unity, to have permanence with Jesus Christ and remain united with Him in heart, mind and will.

May you grow in the faith, maintain a daily devotional life, abide in Christ throughout the day and have a victorious life in Him.

In Christ,

Pastor Craig Caster

Family Discipleship Ministries Presents:

BIBLICAL PRINCIPLES FOR A STRONG FOUNDATION

DISCIPLESHIP WORKBOOK

CRAIG CASTER

For personal, one-to-one and small group study

A LAMP POST BOOK

Family Discipleship Ministries
561 N. Magnolia Avenue
El Cajon, CA 92020
Phone: (619) 590-1901
Fax: (619) 590-1905
Email: info@parentingministry.org
www.parentingministry.org

Biblical Principles for a Strong Foundation
By Craig Caster

Print Version and Electronic Version Copyright © 2001 by Craig Caster
Format and Layout Copyright © 2010 by LAMP POST Inc.
All rights reserved.

Unless otherwise noted:
Scripture quotations taken from the New American Standard Bible®
Copyright © 1960, 1962, 1963, 1968, 1971, 1972, 1973, 1975, 1977, 1995
by The Lockman Foundation
Used by permission.

No part of this book (whether in printed or ebook format, or any other published derivation) may be reproduced in any form without written permission of the publisher or copyright owner except for review purposes. Unauthorized duplication is a violation of applicable laws.

Published By:
LAMP POST INC.
www.lamppostpubs.com

CONTENTS

A LETTER TO THE DISCIPLE 3

Lesson ONE
WHO IS JESUS CHRIST? 7

Lesson TWO
ABUNDANT LIFE IN JESUS CHRIST 16

Lesson THREE
THE FATHERHOOD OF GOD 25

Lesson FOUR
THE HOLY SPIRIT 34

Lesson FIVE
SPIRITUAL GROWTH & MATURITY 43

Lesson SIX
FORGIVENESS & RECONCILIATION 57

Lesson SEVEN
SPIRITUAL WARFARE 72

Lesson EIGHT
END TIMES 85

GLOSSARY
GLOSSARY OF BIBLICAL WORDS AND TERMS 99

LESSON ONE

WHO IS JESUS CHRIST?

If you could roll back the heavens like a scroll, what do you think you would see? The Bible teaches that there are actually three heavens. The first heaven is the immediate atmosphere surrounding us. The second heaven is our solar system, filled with planets, stars and the black unknown. Far beyond lies the third heaven, which the Bible calls *Paradise*. According to the Scriptures, this is the dwelling place or the throne room of God. Several incidents are recorded in the Scriptures where the heavens opened and mortal men were given the privilege of encountering the living God. What they saw and heard altered their perspective and transformed their lives.

Most of us focus mainly on our relationships with others and our daily circumstances. We are often weighed down with the activity, challenges, difficulties and sorrows that accompany this life. Is it possible that our perspectives and our lives could be transformed if we also looked into the heavens and encountered the God who is enthroned above?

The Bible, the Word of God unveils the reality and truths about heaven and God. We learn in the Bible that Jesus Christ, the Son of God is seated on a throne in heaven at the right hand of His Father. Man maintains a variety of views on the identity of Jesus Christ. Some believe Him to be a great prophet, teacher or humanitarian who lived and died long ago, while others see Him as a mystical character from the pages of the Bible. In Matthew 16:15 Jesus Himself addressed His followers with the question, *"Who do you say that I am?"*

The goal of these lessons is to come to know Jesus Christ as He revealed Himself in the Bible and to discover how we can know Him and enter into a life changing relationship with Him.

◆ Did you know that God wants to have a personal relationship with you?
☑ Yes ☐ No

◆ Do you believe that knowing Jesus, and fixing your eyes upon Him can change your life? ☑ Yes ☐ No

DAY 1

JESUS IS OUR CREATOR

Turn in your Bible to the following Scriptures and briefly write out what you learn about Jesus.

> "...I saw the Lord sitting on a throne, lofty and exalted, with the train of His robe filling the temple."
> —Isaiah 6:1

> "Let us fix our eyes on Jesus...who...sat down at the right hand of the throne of God."
> —Hebrews 12:2

> "...I looked, and behold, a door standing open in heaven...and behold, a throne was standing in heaven, and One sitting on the throne... And from the throne proceed flashes of lightning and sounds and peals of thunder..."
> —Revelation 4:1,2,5

> "...he gazed intently into heaven and saw the glory of God..."
> —Acts 7:55

> "All things came into being through Him, and apart from Him nothing came into being that has come into being."
> —John 1:3

WHO IS JESUS CHRIST? | 7

LESSON ONE

Colossians 1:16 _All Things were created by God and For God both on earth + in heaven._

Hebrews 1:10 _God is Creator of both heaven + earth, God has been present from the beginning. Jesus God_

JESUS IS THE SUSTAINER OF OUR LIFE

Christ is not only the wise and powerful creator of all life, He also faithfully sustains His creation.

Sustain — *To hold together, carry, to give support or relief to.*

Turn to Colossians 1:17 and write the verse below.
And he is before all things, and by him all things consist.

According to Hebrews 1:3, how does Jesus hold all things together?
- Brightness of his glory, express image of his glory, Word of his power.

JESUS IS OUR REDEEMER

Two thousand years ago Jesus left His heavenly throne and visited the earth. He who created and sustains life would redeem and become the Savior of the world.

Redeem — *To buy back, to liberate, to recover by payment, to ransom, to rescue, to pay the penalty of, or to purchase or save.*

DAY 2

WHY DID MANKIND NEED A REDEEMER?

The following verses reveal what Jesus saw from His heavenly throne as He looked down upon the earth. Look up the following verses and briefly describe what God saw and how He described mankind.

Genesis 6:5 _Man was wicked continually, hearts were of thoughts of evil._

> "For today in the city of David there has been born for you a Savior, who is Christ the Lord."
> —Luke 2:11

> "... the Son of Man did not come to be served, but to serve, and to give His life a ransom for many."
> —Matthew 20:28

LESSON ONE

Exodus 32:22 _People set on doing evil._

Psalm 14:2-3 _Totally corrupt, not one does good._

✱ Psalm 53:1-3 _Turned toward evil, no good in man._

— _Point you toward God,_

Man was hopelessly lost in sin. From the beginning mankind turned and continues to turn away from the Creator. All of the pain, suffering and sorrows of this life are attributed to man's disobedience to and independence from God.

1st sin = Pride

Sin is...
any offense against God...
exalting oneself against the Creator...
any disobedience of the commandments of God...
putting oneself in His place as the ultimate authority in one's life.

◆ As you look at your life personally and the world around you, do you agree with God's assessment of man? ☑ Yes ☐ No

◆ Do you agree that man's only hope for healing is to turn back to God?
☑ Yes ☐ No

✱ **FOUNDATION TRUTH:** *Jesus Christ is the creator and sustainer of life. He came to earth to redeem mankind.*

"...for all have sinned and fall short of the glory of God."
—Romans 3:23

DAY 3
THE CROSS OF CHRIST

How did Jesus Christ offer man redemption from his state of sin? Turn in your Bible to the Scriptures below for the answer.

Ephesians 1:7 _Redemption through blood, Forgiveness, riches of God's grace._

1 Peter 1:18-19 _Precious blood of Christ,_

"...the Son of Man did not come to be served, but to serve, and to give His life a ransom for many.' "
—Matthew 20:28

LESSON ONE

> "The cross did not happen to Jesus: He came on purpose for it. He is 'the Lamb slain from the foundation of the world'."
> —Oswald Chambers

Death by crucifixion was devised by the Romans and reserved for the lowest criminals. It was a shameful and painfully slow execution. The Bible teaches that Jesus was rejected by His people, forsaken by His friends, and condemned by the religious and government leaders. He was mocked, scourged (beaten on His bare back with a leather whip, containing exposed fragments of metal), His beard was plucked out and His face was spat upon. He was then stripped naked, as the Roman guards gambled for His clothing.

Our Creator was then nailed alive to the cross, where He hung, dying for six agonizing hours. For the first three hours, as He hung on the cross, many passersby mocked, while others wept at the horror. During the final three hours the sky turned black as the holy Father, who cannot look upon sin, turned away from His Son. Jesus was forsaken by His Father, as He laid upon Him the sins of mankind. On that day, over 2,000 years ago, our sins were inserted into His death.

Read John 19:30. What were the final words that Jesus uttered from the cross?
It is Finished.

> "The centre of salvation is the Cross of Jesus, and the reason it is so easy to obtain salvation is because it cost God so much. The Cross is the point where God and sinful man merged with a crash and the way of life is opened —but the crash is on the heart of God."
> —Oswald Chambers

On the cross Jesus Christ finished the work of redemption. According to 2 Corinthians 5:21 what do sinners become when they surrender to Christ?
Righteousness of God in him.

At the cross all of our sins were put on Christ.
At conversion, His righteousness is put on us.
The Innocent paid the penalty.
The guilty are set free!

FOUNDATION TRUTH: Because of our sin we owed God a debt that we could not pay. [Jesus redeemed us and paid our debt by shedding His blood on the cross.]

WHY DID JESUS GO TO THE CROSS?

The author of Psalm 8 was amazed that the Almighty Creator cared for man. Why would Jesus leave the splendor of heaven, become a man, and die a brutal and humiliating death for sinners? The answer is amazing, yet very simple! Look up the following verses to discover why Jesus so willingly went to the cross.

> "When I consider Your heavens, the work of Your fingers, the moon and the stars, which You have set in place, what is man that You are mindful of him, the son of man that you care for him?"
> —Psalm 8:3-4

Romans 5:7-8 _God commendeth his love toward us._

John 3:16 _God so loved the world._

10 | A STRONG FOUNDATION

LESSON ONE

Jesus Christ did not die on the cross in order to establish the Christian *religion*. From His heart of love Jesus paid the highest price so that man could have a *relationship* with God.

SAVED BY GRACE

Rather than turning His anger towards rebellious man, God extended mercy and grace. Read Ephesians 2:1-9 and summarize what you learn.

Dead in sins, God's mercy sent Christ to die for our sins with faith not works we can be saved. Through the gift of salvation on the cross.

"For of His fullness we have all received, and grace upon grace."
—John 1:16

> **Grace** — *God's unearned favor and love; the goodness of God to the undeserving; the forgiveness of sins granted entirely out of the goodness of God, completely apart from any merit on the part of the person forgiven.*

Because God's grace is unearned and undeserved there is nothing we can do to make Him love us more and nothing we can do to make Him love us less. He loves us because He is a God of love. He chooses to love us and desires to have an intimate and personal relationship with those He freely redeemed.

> **Mercy** — *The outward manifestation of pity. It assumes need on the part of him who receives it, and resources adequate to meet the need on the part of him who shows it. It is used of God, who is rich in mercy, kindness or good will toward the miserable and the afflicted and joined with a desire to help them.*

Mercy means that, though we deserved judgement God instead extended His compassion and loving-kindness to us.

"The grace of God is found in His great love for sinners, in His longing to do them good. His Son Jesus Christ personifies grace, for by the offering up of His body, sinners are made whole and pure, once and for all."
—John Bunyan

Salvation is...
deliverance from the power and effects of sin...
liberation from darkness and delusion...
rescue from divine judgement...
preservation from death.

To gain a clearer understanding of the redeeming work of Christ, read the following verses and answer the questions.

How is salvation described In Romans 6:23? *"Gift" through Jesus Christ.*

According to Romans 10:13, who can be saved? *Whoever calls on the name of the Lord.*

Read 1 John 2:2. For whose sins did Jesus die? *All man kind.*

"God's mercy was not increased when Jesus came to earth, it was illustrated! Illustrated in a way we can understand. Jesus knows."
—Eugenia Price

WHO IS JESUS CHRIST? | 11

Propitiate — *To gain or regain the favor or good will of, to appease or conciliate.*

Who does God desire to save? See 1 Timothy 2:4-6. __All Men.__

Jesus Christ died for the sins of the entire human race. He desires all men to call on Him and be saved from judgement and death.

DAY 4

IS JESUS THE ONLY WAY FOR MAN TO BE SAVED?

If we lead a good life, love others or attend church regularly, won't God accept us? Read the following Scriptures and write out what you learn.

Acts 4:12 _____
_____
_____

John 14:6 _____
_____
_____

1 John 5:12 _____
_____
_____

God made provision for man to enter into an intimate relationship with Him. A personal relationship with God is extended to the world, but only on His terms. We must enter in by the blood that Jesus shed on the cross.

> **FOUNDATION TRUTH:** *There is no other way for man to be saved from the penalty of sin except by the grace of God and the sacrifice of Jesus. To reject the cross of Christ is to reject the only means of salvation, thus to remain hopelessly lost and guilty before God.*

HOW DO WE RECEIVE THE GIFT OF SALVATION?

To understand how to receive God's wonderful gift of salvation, read the verses below and write out the main points on the space provided.

Mark 1:15 _____
_____
_____
_____

> *"Knowing God without knowing our own wretchedness makes for pride. Knowing our wretchedness without knowing God makes for despair. Knowing Jesus Christ strikes the balance because He shows us both God and our own wretchedness."*
> —Blaise Pascal

LESSON ONE

Acts 16:30-31 _____
_____
_____

Romans 10:9-10 _____
_____
_____
_____

To receive Christ as your Savior, you simply need to:
- Confess (acknowledge, agree with God) that you are a sinner.
- Repent (feel regret, be sorry) and turn from your sins.
- Ask God to forgive you.
- Invite Jesus Christ to come into your heart and be your Lord and Savior.

Pray the following prayer:

"Lord Jesus, I am a sinner. I need You. Thank You for dying on the cross for me. I open the door of my heart to You and receive You as my Savior and Lord. Thank You for forgiving my sins and giving me eternal life. Take control of my life and make me the person You want me to be. Amen"

◆ Have you believed in Jesus Christ for salvation? ❏ Yes ❏ No

FOUNDATION TRUTH: *God's offer of salvation is free to all who will yield to Him in faith, repent of their sins and ask Christ into their hearts.*

DAY 5
JOY IN HEAVEN

Let's look up into heaven once more. What takes place in heaven when one sinner surrenders his life to Christ?

Luke 15:7 _____
_____
_____

Zephaniah 3:17 _____
_____
_____

Luke 10:20 _____
_____
_____

LESSON ONE

"This shall be written for the generations to come; and the people which shall be created shall praise the Lord. For He hath looked down from the height of His sanctuary; from heaven did the Lord behold the earth; to hear the groaning of the prisoner; to loose those that are appointed to death."
—Psalm 102:18-20

Philippians 4:3-4 _____
_____
_____

Malachi 3:16 _____
_____
_____

DAY 6
WALKING WITH GOD

When we surrender our lives to Christ, we enter into an exciting journey with God. Growing in our relationship with our Creator and Savior is life-changing. As we walk with God, He transforms and blesses our life. Turn in your Bible to the following Scriptures and fill in the blanks below.

Hebrews 2:1 — God is asking me to pay close attention to what I have learned so that I do not _____
_____

Hebrews 4:2 — God is urging me to unite what I have learned with _____
_____
_____

Hebrews 4:16 — God is inviting me to draw near to His throne to receive _____
_____

Hebrews 13:5,6 — God is promising me that He will never _____
_____
_____

"Therefore as you have received Christ Jesus the Lord, so walk in Him, having been firmly rooted and now being built up in Him and established in your faith, just as you were instructed, and overflowing with gratitude."
—Colossians 2:6,7

Take a few moments to reflect on what you have learned in this lesson about God's love for you, His sacrifice for your sins and His desires to have a personal relationship with you. Use the space provided to respond to Him.
_____
_____
_____
_____
_____
_____
_____

DAY 7

Go back through Lesson One and review the four *Foundation Truths* that you learned. Rewrite these truths below.

1) _____
_____
_____

2) _____
_____
_____
_____

3) _____
_____
_____
_____
_____
_____
_____

4) _____
_____
_____
_____

LESSON ONE

"How can I repay the LORD for all his goodness to me? I will lift up the cup of salvation and call on the name of the LORD."
—Psalm 116:12-13

LESSON TWO

ABUNDANT LIFE IN JESUS CHRIST

> "...if any man is in Christ, he is a new creature, the old things passed away; behold, new things have come."
> —2 Corinthians 5:17

> "...I came that they may have life, and have it abundantly."
> —John 10:10b

> "Blessed be the God and Father of our Lord Jesus Christ, who has blessed us with every spiritual blessing in the heavenly places in Christ."
> —Ephesians 1:3

The Bible teaches that believers in Jesus Christ have been given *a new and abundant life* in Him. As we will see in this lesson, Jesus has dealt with the mistakes and failures of our past, made provisions for our present life and promises us a glorious future.

In order to enter into His abundant life we must place our lives completely in God's hands daily, walk in fellowship with Him and abide in His Word. By nature we are independent and self-willed. We must choose daily to deny ourselves, depend on Him and seek His will. He will be faithful to complete the new work he has begun in us and bless us with all spiritual blessings.

DAY 1

THE GARDEN OF EDEN

In the beginning, God created the earth and placed the first man and woman in the Garden of Eden, a perfect environment. The word Eden means *delight* or *pleasure*. God provided everything that Adam and Eve would need. It was His good pleasure and desire to bless them with a happy, abundant, fruitful and satisfying life. God especially wanted to have continued fellowship with them, but something went terribly wrong!

Read Genesis 2:15-17. What one prohibition did God place upon Adam and Eve? What would happen if they disobeyed? _____
_____
_____

> " 'The thief comes only to steal and kill and destroy;...' "
> —John 10:10a

> "Therefore, just as through one man sin entered into the world, and death through sin, and so death spread to all men, because all sinned..."
> —Romans 5:12

As recorded in Genesis, chapter 3, Satan entered the scene, embodied in a serpent. He came as a thief to steal, kill and destroy that which God had intended for Adam and Eve. Satan's first tactic was to tempt Eve to doubt God's goodness.

What did Satan say to Eve in Genesis 3:1? _____
_____

Satan then lied to the woman. What lie did he tell her in Genesis 3:4-5?
_____
_____

When tempted to obey Satan and disobey God, what did the woman do according to Genesis 3:6? _____
_____

LESSON TWO

The first man and woman listened to Satan and doubted the goodness of God. Believing the lie, they were deceived by Satan and sinned against God. The consequences of the fall of man are:

- Man's fellowship with God was broken — *Genesis 3:8-10*
- Mankind was expelled from the garden — *Genesis 3:23-24*
- Death was the judgement for disobedience — *Genesis 5:5*
- Sin was spread through the human race through Adam — *Romans 5:17-19*
- Man was lost, with no hope or means to recover himself — *Ephesians 2:12*

In the beginning God created man in His own image. Like his creator, man possessed a mind capable of logic and rational thinking, a heart to experience emotion and feel love, and a free will. Unfortunately, man exercised his gift of free will to defy his creator. According to Genesis 5:1-3, after sin entered the earth, what image did man bear?_____

"God created man in His own image, in the image of God He created him; male and female He created them."
—Genesis 1:27

FELLOWSHIP WITH GOD RESTORED

Through the sacrifice of Jesus Christ on the cross, God provided mankind's only hope of being saved from the penalty of sin and death. Our fellowship with God can only be restored through the cross.

Read Romans 5:12-21 and summarize what you learned.
_____
_____
_____

Transgression — *To pass beyond a boundary; to violate or break a law or command.*
Condemnation — *To be pronounced guilty or deserving punishment.*
Righteous — *Innocent, conformity to law, to be absolved or acquitted from guilt.*

"But the free gift is not like the transgression. For if by the transgression of the one the many died, much more did the grace of God and the gift by the grace of the one Man, Jesus Christ, abound to the many."
—Romans 5:15

DAY 2

THE BLESSINGS OF KNOWING GOD

In Lesson One we learned that the salvation is received by faith in Jesus Christ. Salvation means that we are saved or delivered from the power and effects of sin. In addition, we are born again, justified, adopted into God's family and granted eternal life.

● BELIEVERS ARE BORN AGAIN

Born Again — *Renewal or spiritual rebirth.*

Read John 3:1-8. What did Jesus tell Nicodemus he must do in order to enter the kingdom of God?_____
_____

"Blessed be the God and Father of our Lord Jesus Christ, who according to His great mercy has caused us to be born again to a living hope through the resurrection of Jesus Christ from the dead."
—1 Peter 1:3

ABUNDANT LIFE IN JESUS CHRIST | 17

LESSON TWO

"...He has granted to us His precious and magnificent promises, in order that by them you might become partakers of the divine nature, having escaped the corruption that is in the world by lust."
—2 Peter 1:4

Read Ephesians 2:1-5. What does Christ do for us when He saves us by His grace (verse 5)? _____
_____

When we surrender our lives to Jesus Christ we are born of the Spirit or, *born again*. God's Holy Spirit comes to dwell within our hearts and gives us new life, His life. He promises that He will never leave us or forsake us (Hebrews 13:5). The Holy Spirit imparts to us the very nature of God.

Because God has given us new life it is His will that we reject anything from our past that does not edify us or glorify Him. Removing the old and imparting the new is a gradual and on-going process that God brings us through as we walk with Him.

"For I am confident of this very thing, that He who began a good work in you will perfect it until the day of Christ Jesus."
—Philippians 1:6

◆ Are you willing to participate with God in this process and surrender all to Him? ❑ Yes ❑ No

◆ As you reflect on your own life, is there anything that God has revealed to you that is hindering you from fully committing your life to Him? ❑ Yes ❑ No

Explain. _____
_____

> **FOUNDATION TRUTH:** *When we surrender our lives to Jesus Christ we are born of the Spirit and given new life.*

● **BELIEVERS ARE JUSTIFIED**

Justification... just as if I had never sinned.

Justify — *To declare righteous, to pardon and absolve from guilt and punishment.*

In Romans 3:23-26 we read that God is, *"just and the justifier of the one who has faith in Jesus."* From verse 25, what did Jesus do with the sins we previously committed? _____
_____

"The wisdom of God has ordained a way for the love of God to deliver us from the wrath of God without compromising the justice of God!"
—John Piper

Rewrite the blessing given in Romans 4:7-8.
_____
_____
_____
_____

Read Colossians 2:13-14. What did God do with our debt of sin?
_____
_____

LESSON TWO

FOUNDATION TRUTH: *When we surrender our lives to Jesus Christ our sins are forgiven and we are declared righteous in Christ.*

DAY 3

- **BELIEVERS ARE ADOPTED INTO GOD'S FAMILY**

    Adopt — *To choose, to take up, to embrace; to take as one's own what is another's.*

God not only gives us new life and forgives all of our sins, but He also adopts us into His family, making us His own children.

Read John 1:12 and 1 John 3:1 and write what you learn about your adoption into God's family. _____
_____
_____

Read Psalm 103:13. How does God look upon His children? _____
_____

We have a good Heavenly Father, who is full of patience, love and kindness for us. Because He created us, He knew us before we knew Him. In fact, He knows us better than we know ourselves. The depth of His love toward us is beyond our understanding. The Scriptures provide a clear portrait of the Father-heart of God in the story of the prodigal son. Turn in your Bible to Luke 15:11-24 and answer the following questions.

When the son came to his senses, what did he remember about his father? (verse 17) _____
_____

How did the son plan to approach his father? (verse 18 and 19) _____
_____
_____

How did the father receive him? (verse 20-24) _____
_____
_____

Read Hebrews 12:5-10. As our Heavenly Father, what will God do in our lives?
_____
_____

"The Spirit Himself testifies with our spirit that we are children of God,"
—Romans 8:16

"He predestined us to adoption as sons through Jesus Christ to Himself, according to the kind intention of His will."
—Ephesians 1:5

"...He disciplines us for our good, so that we may share His holiness. All discipline for the moment seems not to be joyful, but sorrowful; yet to those who have been trained by it, afterwards it yields the peaceful fruit of righteousness."
—Hebrews 12:10-11

ABUNDANT LIFE IN JESUS CHRIST | 19

LESSON TWO

Discipline — *Training, which includes teaching, instruction, chastening and correction.*

God begins a new work in His adopted children to train, teach and instill the family likeness in us. We will study His training process in Lesson Three.

One of the blessings of being a child of God is that we now become heirs of all that He possesses. Read the following verses to discover the riches of our inheritance.

Psalm 50:10-12 _____

Haggai 2:8 _____

Read 1 Peter 1:4. Where is our inheritance? _____

How should the fact that you are an adopted child of God influence the way you see yourself? _____

"I pray that the eyes of your heart may be enlightened, so that you will know what is the hope of His calling, what are the riches of the glory of His inheritance in the saints."
—Ephesians 1:18

FOUNDATION TRUTH: *When we surrender our lives to Christ our Heavenly Father adopts us into His family, making us His own children.*

DAY 4

- **BELIEVERS ARE GIVEN THE GIFT OF ETERNAL LIFE**

    Eternal - *Everlasting, unending.*

    As we saw in Day One of this lesson, the punishment for Adam and Eve's rebellion was death. Jesus reversed the death sentence by taking upon Himself the punishment for man's sin, and granting eternal life to all who would believe in Him. Read the wonderful promises from John 3:16 and John 11:25-26 and briefly write out what you learn.

    _____
    _____
    _____
    _____

    Read 1 John 5:11-13, then rewrite verse 12 in your own words. _____
    _____
    _____
    _____

"For the wages of sin is death, but the free gift of God is eternal life in Christ Jesus our Lord."
—Romans 6:23

It is difficult for us to understand the gift of eternal life because of the reality that all men die a physical death. As Christians, though our physical bodies die from illness, old age or accident, our spirits are immortal and will never die. In fact, we will be resurrected and given a new heavenly body that will not be subject to illness, old age or death! The Bible is the best teacher. What truths about eternal life do you learn from the following verses?

1 Corinthians 15:35-58 _____
_____
_____
_____

Because God's plan for our lives extends throughout eternity, we ought to cease striving for complete fulfillment in the things of this life. God desires to bless our lives in this world, yet absolute happiness and fulfillment will not be fully attained until we arrive at our eternal destination in the presence of our Heavenly Father and our Savior, Jesus Christ.

> **FOUNDATION TRUTH:** *When we surrender our lives to Christ, we are granted the precious gift of eternal life.*

Jesus came to earth to restore mankind to the blessed condition that God originally intended. In Him we are born again to new life, granted forgiveness for our sins, adopted into God's family and given eternal life.

DAY 5

THE ENEMY

Satan continues to come against God's people, just as he did in the Garden of Eden, attempting to rob us of God's blessings. His tactics have not changed. Satan's weapons are temptations, deceptions (calling evil good and good evil), condemnation and lies. Read the following verses and fill in the blanks.

Matthew 4:3 — Satan is _____

- He wants to ensnare us in sin as he did before the Spirit of God faithfully took up residence in our hearts.

2 Corinthians 11:3 — Satan is _____

- He wants to seduce and deceive us, leading us astray from devotion to the Father, who has mercifully adopted us.

Revelation 12:9,10 — Satan is _____

LESSON TWO

"But our citizenship is in heaven. And we eagerly await a Savior from there, the Lord Jesus Christ, who, by the power that enables Him to bring everything under His control, will transform our lowly bodies so that they will be like His glorious body."
—Philippians 3:20-21

"The God of peace will crush Satan under your feet."
—Romans 16:20

LESSON TWO

- He wants to fill our minds with guilt and regret over past failures and mistakes, as well as hopelessness about our future.

John 8:44 — Satan is _____

- He wants to enslave us in deception and a multitude of fears.

◆ Has Satan been using any of these tactics on you? ❏ Yes ❏ No

Explain _____
_____
_____
_____

DAY 6

● **COMBATING THE ENEMY**

What does the Bible instruct us to do when we are attacked by our enemy?

1 Peter 5:6-9 _____
_____
_____

James 4:7-10 _____
_____
_____

"Then He will also say to those on His left, "Depart from Me, accursed ones, into the eternal fire which has been prepared for the devil and his angels."
—Matthew 25:41

Satan does not flee because he fears us, but because He fears our God. Turn in your Bible to James 2:19. What do demons do in God's presence? _____
_____
_____

Satan is not equal in power to God. He is a created being who will ultimately and finally be destroyed by God. What two titles are ascribed to God in Psalm 91:1?
_____
_____

In the Old Testament we learn of Satan's attack upon Job, a righteous man. Though Satan brought destruction into his life, who was in control of Job, his circumstances and Satan? Read Job 1:7-12 and 2:1-6 _____

According to Luke 22:31-34 who did Satan have to go through before he could assault Peter? _____

22 | A STRONG FOUNDATION

LESSON TWO

Jesus said His followers are like sheep, and He is their shepherd. Like sheep we are defenseless against thieves and predators if we wander from our shepherd's side. God calls us to *draw near* to Him, not only for protection from our enemies, but also because He longs to have fellowship with us.

> **FOUNDATION TRUTH:** *Though we have a powerful enemy we have an all-powerful God who exercises absolute authority over Satan and guarantees our safety as we put our trust in Him.*

FELLOWSHIP WITH GOD

Fellowship — *Companionship and company; friendly relationship; a union of peers or friends; the habitual sharing, the constant giving to, and receiving from each other.*

God desires an intimate relationship with us. He saved us from our fallen condition and delivered us from our enemy so that we might have a relationship and fellowship with Him. We participate in this relationship in the following ways:

◆ **PRAYER** — Prayer is more than simply asking God to do something for us or to give us something. The following acronym (ACTS) is an easy way to remember the different aspects of prayer.

Adoration — worshiping and praising God for who He is; remembering His goodness, loving kindness, mercy, patience, etc. (Jude 1:24-25).

Confession — admitting our faults and failures to Him and receiving His forgiveness (1 John 1:9).

Thanksgiving — recalling His goodness and the blessings He has bestowed upon us (Hebrews 13:15).

Supplication — placing all of our needs before Him, fully trusting Him to respond and meet our needs according to His will (Philippians 4:6-7).

◆ **READING GOD'S WORD** — We come to know God more intimately, understand His ways, and align ourselves with His plans through reading, meditating upon and obeying His Word (Psalm 119:105).

◆ **CHURCH ATTENDANCE** — Consistently receiving the spoken word from the pastor and worshipping with the congregation helps us grow and provides opportunities to serve (Hebrews 10:24-25).

"I am the good shepherd; the good shepherd lays down His life for the sheep."
—John 10:11

"God is faithful, through whom you were called into fellowship with His Son, Jesus Christ our Lord."
—1 Corinthians 1:9

"Let us therefore draw near with confidence to the throne of grace, that we may receive mercy and may find grace to help in time of need."
—Hebrews 4:16

> *Therefore, my brother who wants to learn to abide in Jesus, take time each day, before you read, while you read and after you read, to put yourself into living contact with the living Jesus, to yield yourself distinctly and consciously to His blessed influence, so will you give Him the opportunity of taking hold of you, of drawing you up and keeping you safe in His almighty life.*
> —Andrew Murray

LESSON TWO

◆ **DISCIPLESHIP** — Meeting on a regular basis with a more mature believer for the purpose of accountability and encouragement in your spiritual growth and personal relationship with the Savior (Matthew 28:19, Titus 2:1-5), then, in time, discipling a younger believer.

◆ **FELLOWSHIP WITH OTHER BELIEVERS** — Spending time with others who love Jesus is very important to your growth as a Christian. (Psalm 119:63)

DAY 7

Go back through Lesson Two and review the five *Foundation Truths* that you learned. Rewrite these truths below.

1) _____
_____
_____
_____

2) _____
_____
_____
_____

3) _____
_____
_____
_____

4) _____
_____
_____
_____

5) _____
_____
_____
_____

LESSON THREE

THE FATHERHOOD OF GOD

DAY 1

OUR HEAVENLY FATHER

Among many people the term *father* does not evoke fond feelings. Instead, they have known only harsh fathers, who have been unable or unwilling to parent them as God intended. Other fathers, rather than being harsh, are weak or passive and have disregarded the love and training that God's Word says a father should give his children. Many simply neglect the responsibility altogether and abandon their families.

The Bible assures us that through Christ and His redeeming work, our creator adopts us and becomes our Father. As we will see in this lesson, our Heavenly Father is a perfect parent, faithful in His love and care, skillful to train, wise to guide, always available and committed to raise us up to maturity.

It has often been said that *"we are all God's children."* However, the Bible clearly teaches that though we are all God's *creation*, the Fatherhood of God is not universal. Read the following Scriptures and note what you learn about who has the *right* to call God *'Father.'*

> *" 'Father' is the Christian's name for God."*
> —J.I. Packer

John 1:12 _____
_____
_____

Galatians 3:26 _____
_____
_____

Ephesians 2:18-19 _____
_____
_____

> **FOUNDATION TRUTH:** Only those who have surrendered their lives to Christ can rightly address God as their Father. God sent His Son to redeem us, forgive our sins and adopt us as His own children.

DAY 2

A FATHER WHO KNOWS

Because our Heavenly Father is also our creator, He absolutely knows and understands us uniquely and individually. In the following Bible verses, you will learn how intimately acquainted God is with you personally.

Psalm 22:9-10 _____
_____
_____

Psalm 71:6 _____
_____
_____

Psalm 103:13-14 _____
_____
_____

Psalm 139:1-18 _____
_____
_____

God not only knew you before you were born, He chose your parents and uniquely formed you in your mother's womb. He has ordained circumstances in your life, whether joyous or difficult, to bring you to a place where you would seek Him. Though you did not know or acknowledge Him, He has watched over you and patiently waited for you to seek Him.

"... He made from one man every nation of mankind to live on all the face of the earth, having determined their appointed times and the boundaries of their habitation, that they would seek God, if perhaps they might grope for Him and find Him, though He is not far from each one of us."
—Acts 17:26-27

DAY 3
GOD'S TRAINING METHODS

As a loving Father, God desires His children to grow into strong, healthy, mature adulthood. He wants us to share His attitudes, His view of life and to bear the *family image*, to be like Christ. To accomplish this, the Bible teaches that God disciplines us.

> **Discipline** — *Training intended to elicit a specified pattern of behavior to educate and instill character.*

Read Hebrews 12:5-11 and answer the following questions:

Who does the Lord discipline? (v. 6) _____

What does this discipline prove? (v. 8) _____

Why does He discipline us? (v. 10) _____

What result does discipline yield? (v. 11) _____

LESSON THREE

Before we came to Christ we were *spiritual orphans*. We were self-centered and in the habit of indulging in sinful behavior. After we accepted Christ, God patiently and persistently set about to purge us of the thoughts, attitudes and actions that were not pleasing to Him, and replacing them with the *"peaceful fruit of righteousness."*

Read Galatians 5:22-23 and list the *fruit* that God will produce in our lives.

_____
_____
_____

"I will not leave you as orphans; I will come to you."
—John 14:18

As a wise Father, God has effective methods for training His children. He knows each of us intimately and understands our uniqueness. We should take great comfort in the knowledge that, though others may not understand us, our loving Heavenly Father does. God understands our temperament – the weaknesses, strengths and limitations of our personality. He also knows the temptations that accost us. God knows what gives us great joy and what brings us deep sorrow. He wisely takes all this into consideration as He works out His will in our individual lives.

It is true that God loves us just as we are, but it is equally true that, because He loves us, He will not leave us the way we are. He longs for us to share His holiness and to be transformed into the likeness of His Son!

> *"But we all, with unveiled face beholding as in a mirror the glory of the Lord, are being transformed into the same image from glory to glory…"*
> —2 Corinthians 3:18

"God's promises us forgiveness for what we have done, but we need His deliverance from what we are"
—Corrie ten Boom

Transform — *To change a thing into another or from one form to another, metamorphose.*

◆ Are you willing to yield fully to the Heavenly Father in this process of transformation? ❏ Yes ❏ No

DAY 4

GOD'S TOOLS FOR TRANSFORMATION

As a potter has special tools to shape and mold a piece of clay into a beautiful vessel, God, like a master potter, has tools to shape and mold our lives. If we will yield to His gentle and firm touch in our lives, He will reshape us into individuals of inner strength and beauty. Let's look at the three primary tools God uses in His transformation process; the Bible, our trials and difficulties, and other people.

"But now, O Lord, Thou art our Father, we are the clay, and Thou our potter; and all of us are the work of Thy hand."
—Isaiah 64:8

● **THE BIBLE**

We learn the foundational truths of our faith and grow in that faith from daily reading of the Word of God. Read the verses below and fill in the blanks.

THE FATHERHOOD OF GOD | 27

LESSON THREE

"All Scripture is inspired by God and profitable for teaching, for reproof, for correction, for training in righteousness..."
—2 Timothy 3:16

Psalm 119:105 — God's Word is a _____

Hebrews 4:12 — The Word of God is _____

Jeremiah 23:29 — God's Word is like _____

Job 23:12 — God's Word is to be treasured more than _____

Ephesians 5:26 — God's Word sanctifies and _____

1 Peter 2:2 — God's Word _____

What truths have you learned from God's Word that have influenced the way you feel, think, or desire to live your life? _____

As we read the Word our goal should not be to simply acquire Bible knowledge. Rather, our pursuit should and must be to know Jesus more intimately. Turn in your Bible to John 5:38-40. Why did Jesus reprove the religious Jews?
_____

> *"We must study His words, fairly devour His words, let them sink into our thought and into our heart, keep them in our memory, obey them constantly in our life, let them shape and mold our daily life and our every act. This is really the method of abiding in Christ. It is through His words that Jesus imparts Himself to us."*
> — R.A. Torrey

FOUNDATION TRUTH: *The Word of God is a powerful tool that God will use to transform our lives.*

● OUR TRIALS AND THE DIFFICULTIES OF LIFE

Our Heavenly Father uses our difficulties to teach us, to mature our faith in Him and to bring us to a place of spiritual abundance. In the midst of our trials, we must rest in His grace, love and tender care. We need to have God's perspective or we will become broken or hardened by our trials.

What does God's Word say about our trials and difficult circumstances?

James 1:2-4 _____

> *"Teach me to treat all that comes to me with peace of soul and with firm conviction that Your will governs all. In unforeseen events let me not forget that all are sent by You."*
> —Elisabeth Elliot

28 | A STRONG FOUNDATION

LESSON THREE

1 Peter 1:6-7 _____
_____
_____

Psalm 66:10-12 _____
_____
_____

Recall a situation in your life, presently or in the past when the Lord used difficult or painful circumstances to bring you closer to Him.
_____
_____
_____
_____

FOUNDATION TRUTH: *If we are willing, God will use our trials to transform us into the image of His Son.*

● **OTHER PEOPLE**

God places other people in our lives to counsel and encourage us, or, through disappointing experiences, to teach us to put our confidence in Him alone. What do you learn about others in the following verses?

Proverbs 27:17 _____
_____
_____

Romans 1:11-12 _____
_____
_____

Psalm 41:9-12 _____
_____
_____

2 Timothy 4:16-17 _____
_____
_____

What people has God put in your life to encourage you in your faith, or challenges you to be patient and loving? _____
_____
_____
_____

THE FATHERHOOD OF GOD | 29

LESSON THREE

"Be content to be a child, and let the Father proportion out daily to thee what light, what power, what exercises, what straits, what fears, what troubles He sees fit for thee"
—Isaac Penington (1610-1679)

DAY 5

THE PROMISES OF GOD'S TENDER CARE

Our Heavenly Father is ready to assume full responsibility for the life wholly yielded and devoted to Him. We are surrounded by His watchful care. Read the following verses and fill in the blanks.

Psalm 91:4 — Above us are His _____

Deuteronomy 33:27 — Under us are His _____

Psalm 34:7 — We are surrounded by _____

Philippians 4:6-7 — Our hearts and minds are guarded by _____
_____

In the following section, we will immerse ourselves in the truths of our Heavenly Father's promises to care for us.

● THE PROMISE OF GOD'S PRESENCE

Read the following Scriptures and briefly write what you learn about God's constant nearness to us.

Psalm 23:4 _____
_____
_____

Psalm 121:1-5 _____
_____
_____

Psalm 139:7-10 _____
_____
_____

Hebrews 13:5-6 _____
_____
_____

"...I am with you always, even to the end of the age.'"
—Matthew 28:20

As God's children, we should never feel alone. Our Father is ever watchful and always near.

FOUNDATION TRUTH: *In His tender care, our Heavenly Father is always with us.*

LESSON THREE

● **THE PROMISE OF GOD'S PROVISION**

What do the following verses teach you about trusting God as your provider?

Matthew 6:25-26 _____
_____
_____

Romans 8:32 _____
_____
_____

Philippians 4:19 _____
_____
_____

In Matthew 6:9 how did Jesus instruct His disciples to address God in prayer?
_____

From Matthew 7:7-11, what will the Father give to those who ask?_____
_____

God knows what is best for us and gives only good gifts to His children. Out of His love and wisdom He often withholds from us what we ask, and instead He gives what He knows is best for us. These are opportunities for us to trust in His wisdom and goodness, though we don't always understand His ways!

Read Matthew 6:24-34. If God cares for the birds, whose Father He is not, we must believe that He will certainly take care of us, His beloved children. (Note in verse 32, the *gentiles* refer to those that do not know God.)

Do you currently have worries, concerns or cares?   ❑ Yes   ❑ No

Explain. _____
_____
_____

According to Matthew 6:33, what is the remedy for worrying?
_____
_____

We must make seeking God and our personal relationship with Him our first priority. As we develop the habit of committing everything to Him, and trusting Him in all things, He will enable us to overcome the sinful habit of worrying!

"Every good thing given and every perfect gift is from above, coming down from the Father of lights, with whom there is no variation or shifting shadow."
—James 1:17

"Therefore humble yourselves under the mighty hand of God, that He may exalt you at the proper time, casting all your anxiety on Him, because He cares for you."
—1 Peter 5:6-7

LESSON THREE

FOUNDATION TRUTH: *In His tender care, our Heavenly Father will meet all of our needs.*

● **THE PROMISE OF GOD'S PROTECTION**

The Bible contains 365 commands to fear not. As children of the Almighty God, we can rest secure in Him. Read the following Scriptures and write out what you learn about God's protection of you.

1 Peter 1:5 _____
_____
_____

Psalm 91:11,12 _____
_____
_____

Psalm 121:5-8 _____
_____
_____

"For it is you who blesses the righteous man, O LORD, you surround him with favor as with a shield."
—Psalm 5:12

FOUNDATION TRUTH: *In His tender care, our Heavenly Father guards and keeps us.*

DAY 6
A FATHER WHO CARES

Our Heavenly Father goes to great lengths in His Word to assure us of His discipline, protection and provision. We must respond in faith and entrust our lives and all of our concerns into His keeping. While God's glory, power and sovereignty are demonstrated in His creation, the depth of His divine character is demonstrated in His Fatherhood. God's love, patience, kindness, mercy, and goodness are revealed in His relationship with us, His children! Look up the following verses in your Bible and write out what you learn about the character of our Heavenly Father.

1 John 3:1 _____
_____
_____

2 Peter 3:9 _____
_____
_____

"See how great a love the Father has bestowed on us, that we would be called children of God; and such we are. For this reason the world does not know us, because it did not know Him."
—1 John 3:1

LESSON THREE

Ephesians 1:5 _____
_____
_____

2 Corinthians 1:3 _____
_____
_____

1 Peter 1:3 _____
_____
_____

DAY 7

Go back through Lesson Three and review the six **Foundation Truths** that you learned. Rewrite these truths below.

1) _____
_____
_____

2) _____
_____
_____

3) _____
_____
_____

4) _____
_____

5) _____
_____
_____

6) _____
_____
_____

LESSON FOUR

> "...when you believed in Christ, he identified you as his own by giving you the Holy Spirit, whom he promised long ago. The Spirit is God's guarantee that he will give us everything he promised and that he has purchased us to be his own people. This is just one more reason for us to praise our glorious God."
> —Ephesians 1:13-14 (NLT)

THE HOLY SPIRIT

In this lesson, we will study the biblical teaching on the Holy Spirit. This study is intended to clarify who the Holy Spirit is and give understanding of the wonderful work He desires to do in the lives of every child of God.

DAY 1

WHO IS THE HOLY SPIRIT?

Unfortunately, there is much confusion on the subject of the Holy Spirit. Many believe that the Holy Spirit is an *influence* emanating from God or a *power* that God imparts to the Christian. However, the Bible clearly teaches that the Holy Spirit, in union with the Father and the Son form the Trinity of God. The Holy Spirit is equal in power and glory with the Father and the Son. The Father and the Son operate through the Holy Spirit.

Like the Father and the Son, the Holy Spirit is eternal, omnipresent (in all places at all times), omnipotent (all-powerful) and omniscient (all-knowing). Read the following Scriptures that describe the Holy Spirit and fill in the blanks.

Hebrews 9:14 — The Holy Spirit is _____

Psalm 139:7-10 — The Holy Spirit is _____

Luke 1:35 — The Holy Spirit is _____

1 Corinthians 2:10-11 — The Holy Spirit is _____

The Holy Spirit possesses defined personality traits. People often refer to the Holy Spirit as 'It,' but as you will see from the following Scriptures, the Holy Spirit is a divine person.

- He has a will — 1 Corinthians 12:11
- He loves — Romans 15:30
- He grieves — Ephesians 4:30
- He can be lied to — Acts 5:3
- He jealously desires us — James 4:5
- He can be quenched or suppressed — 1 Thessalonians 5:19
- He is insulted by man's rejection of the Savior — Hebrews 10:29
- He speaks — 1 Timothy 4:1
- He is the truth — 1 John 5:6

> "Do you know, my friends, that the Spirit within you is very God? Oh that our eyes were opened to see the greatness of God's gift! Oh that we might realize the vastness of the resources secreted in our own hearts! I could shout with joy as I think, 'The Spirit who dwells within me is no mere influence, but a living Person; He is very God. The infinite God is within my heart!'"
> —Watchman Nee

FOUNDATION TRUTH: *The Holy Spirit is our Comforter in all of our difficulties, our ever-present Companion, our Convicter in times of temptation, and our Counselor when we need guidance and wisdom.*

DAY 2

THE HOLY SPIRIT GIVES NEW BIRTH

Jesus Christ wanted His followers to understand the regenerating work of the Holy Spirit. Turn in your Bible to John 3 and read His words in verses 1-8.

What did Jesus tell Nicodemus he must do in order to see the Kingdom of God?
_____

Jesus taught that every man and woman must experience two births in order to go to heaven; a *physical* birth (water) and a *spiritual* birth (by the Spirit).

To help Nicodemus understand the Holy Spirit, Jesus likened Him and His work to the wind in verse 8.

- The wind blows where it wills, likewise the Spirit is sovereign and free, and no man controls Him. He works as *He* wills.

- The wind is invisible, yet powerful. You cannot see the wind, but its effects are visible. In like manner, the Holy Spirit is invisible, but evidence of His power is visible in individual's lives and situations.

- Finally, as air is life giving, so also the Holy Spirit gives life.

Turn in your Bible to the following verses and write what you learn about the work of the Holy Spirit in our lives.

John 6:63 _____
_____
_____

Titus 3:5 _____
_____
_____

1 Corinthians 6:19 _____
_____
_____

"For you have been born again not of seed which is perishable but imperishable, that is through the living and enduring word of God."
—1 Peter 1:23

THE HOLY SPIRIT | 35

LESSON FOUR

"But we all, with unveiled face, beholding as in a mirror the glory of the Lord, are being transformed into the same image from glory to glory, just as from the Lord, the Spirit."
—2 Corinthians 3:18

"...you have purified your souls in obeying the truth through the Spirit ..."
—1Peter 1:22

HOLY SPIRIT TRANSFORMS OUR LIFE

The Holy Spirit, invisible, yet powerful, comes to dwell in the hearts of all believers, imparting to us new life. We cannot see Him, yet the effects of His presence are visible in our lives. It is His work to transform each believer to the image of Christ. Read the following Scriptures about the Spirit and write out what you learn.

2 Peter 1:3-4 _____
_____
_____

Ezekiel 36:26-27 _____
_____
_____

1 Corinthians 2:12-16 _____
_____
_____

"...that He would grant you, according to the riches of His glory, to be strengthened with power through His Spirit in the inner man..."
—Ephesians 3:16

One aspect of the Good News of the Christian faith is that God is not asking us to reform or improve *ourselves*. By the indwelling Holy Spirit, God will conform and change us *from the inside out!* We participate in this process in transformation as we daily seek intimacy with Him. As we draw near to God in devotion and quiet time He gives us His heart, mind and His very nature. We must daily,

Surrender — *to undergo capture, to submit to the power of another.*
Cooperate — *to work together toward a common end.*
Yield — *give in, relinquish.*
Submit — *obey.*

> ***FOUNDATION TRUTH:*** *The Holy Spirit comes to dwell within each believer, to impart new life and to transform us into the image of Christ.*

DAY 3

"But when the Helper comes, whom I shall send to you from the Father, the Spirit of truth who proceeds from the Father, He will testify of Me."
—John 15:26

THE HOLY SPIRIT IS OUR HELPER

Hours before Jesus was arrested and crucified, He took His disciples to the upper room to partake of the last supper with Him, and to teach them. This teaching is contained in chapters 13-17 of the Gospel of John. Among many other topics of importance to Jesus, He taught His followers about the Holy Spirit, whom He would send to them after He ascended to heaven. Read the following references in John and list what you learn about the Holy Spirit, our Helper.

LESSON FOUR

John 14:16-27 _____
_____
_____

John 15:26 _____
_____
_____

John 16:7-15 _____
_____
_____

Jesus told the disciples that the Holy Spirit would be *another* Helper, who would be *with* them and *in* them.

Read the Scriptures below and write out what the Holy Spirit does to help us.

Romans 8:26-27, Jude 20 - The Holy Spirit helps us _____
_____

Romans 8:14, John 16:13 - The Holy Spirit is our _____
_____

1 John 2:27, John 14:26 - The Holy Spirit is our _____
_____

Luke 12:11-12 - The Holy Spirit teaches us _____
_____

DAY 4

THE FULLNESS OF THE SPIRIT

As we yield to the Holy Spirit He fills us. In Ephesians 5:18 this filling is compared to being intoxicated. As an individual consumes wine, they become influenced, affected and even controlled by the alcohol. In a similar manner, as we surrender to the Holy Spirit He is able to influence, affect and control us. As He purifies our thoughts, motives and desires, He is able also to transform our actions and behavior.

Turn in your Bible to John 7:37-39. In verse 37, what two things does Jesus ask the spiritually thirsty to do? _____
_____

From verse 38, what will then flow from their lives? _____

> *"...the Spirit also helps our weakness..."*
> —Romans 8:26

> *"So we may boldly say: 'The Lord is my helper; I will not fear. What can man do to me?'"*
> —Hebrews 13:6

> *"Why is it that some of God's children live victorious lives while others are in a state of constant defeat? The difference is not accounted for by the presence or absence of the Spirit (for He dwells in the heart of every child of God) but by this, that some recognize His indwelling and other do not. True revelation of the fact of the Spirit's indwelling will revolutionize the life of any Christian."*
> —Watchman Nee

> *"And do not get drunk with wine, for that is dissipation, but be filled with the Spirit."*
> —Ephesians 5:18

THE HOLY SPIRIT | 37

LESSON FOUR

As we acknowledge our need (thirst), believe in Jesus and receive (drink) from Him, He will fill us to overflowing. His life will fill and overflow in us!

According to Jeremiah 2:13, what two evils did Israel commit? _____
_____
_____

"For My people have committed two evils: they have forsaken me, the fountain of living waters, to hew for themselves cisterns, broken cisterns that can hold no water."
—Jeremiah 2:13

Rather than trusting God to fill them and meet their needs, the children of Israel abandoned Him, and sought out other sources of satisfaction and fulfillment. God told them that these methods would not *hold water* to Him!

● **THE FRUIT OF THE SPIRIT**

The Holy Spirit jealously desires our devotion. He is a gentleman and will not trespass our will or force our obedience. Jesus voluntarily offered Himself as a sacrifice for our sins. In turn, repentant, forgiven sinners should respond by voluntarily surrendering to Him. As we yield daily to the Spirit, He will fill us up to overflowing. His living water will flow from within and produce fruit in our lives.

" 'The Spirit who dwells in us yearns jealously'..."
—James 4:5b (NKJ)

This fruit is described in Galatians 5:22-23. List the fruit below.
_____
_____

What specific fruit of the Spirit has been lacking in your life?
_____
_____

"Abide in Me, and I in you. As the branch cannot bear fruit of itself, unless it abides in the vine, so neither can you unless you abide in Me."
—John 15:4

The measure of the Spirit's fruit in our life is directly related to our degree of dependence upon Him. Just as a fruit tree requires sunshine, water and healthy soil to produce fruit, the child of God must be absolutely dependent upon the Holy Spirit to bear the fruit of the Spirit.

◆ Are you willing to surrender all to God and trust Him to reproduce His life in you? ❏ Yes ❏ No

● **THE GIFTS OF THE SPIRIT**

The Holy Spirit not only produces the fruit of the Spirit in our lives, He also imparts spiritual gifts to us. The gifts of the Spirit cannot be earned. They are not merits for faithful service but graces from God. They are not related to our natural abilities, personalities or character traits. Three chapters of the New Testament are devoted exclusively to the teaching of the spiritual gifts. Read 1 Corinthians 12-14.

"If you then, being evil, know how to give good gifts to your children, how much more shall your heavenly Father give the Holy Spirit to those who ask Him?"
—Luke 11:13

According to 1 Corinthians 12:7,11 to which members of the body of Christ will the Holy Spirit impart spiritual gifts? _____

What should be the main objective for exercising spiritual gifts (1 Corinthians 14:12,26b)?
_____

Edification — *The act of building a structure. To instruct, improve or build up spiritually.*

What results when the gifts of the Spirit are exercised with pride, selfishness or without love for the brethren? See 1 Corinthians 13:1,2 _____
_____

Because of the potential abuse in exercising the gifts of the Spirit, many Christians and evangelical churches avoid the subject altogether. What words of warning does Paul give in 1 Corinthians 12:1 concerning the gifts? _____
_____

The gifts of the Spirit are listed in 1 Corinthians 12:8-10,28.

1. Word of Wisdom - Acts 6:10
2. Word of knowledge - 1 Corinthians 1:5, Romans 15:14
3. Special faith - Acts 3:1-16
4. Gifts of healings - Mark 6:13, James 5:14-16
5. Operations of miracles - Acts 5:12-15, Hebrews 2:4
6. Prophecy - Exodus 7:1,2, Jeremiah 1:9, 1 Corinthians 14:1-5,24,25,39
7. Discerning of spirits - Acts 13:9-11, Hebrews 5:14
8. Tongues - 1 Corinthians 14:1-5, Acts 2:3-11, Romans 8:26,27
9. Interpretation of tongues - 1 Corinthians 14:13,27,28
10. Helps - Acts 20:35
11. Governments - 1 Timothy 5:17

◆ The gifts of the Spirit are distributed to each member of the body of Christ. Do you know your gifts? ❏ Yes ❏ No

Explain. _____
_____

FOUNDATION TRUTH: As we yield to the Holy Spirit, He produces spiritual fruit and imparts spiritual gifts to us.

DAY 5

EMPOWERED BY THE HOLY SPIRIT

The Holy Spirit is *with* and *in* each believer to reproduce the life of Jesus in us. The term *Christian* actually means *little Christ*. Our goal is to become like Jesus.

"And He gave some as apostles, and some as prophets, and some as evangelists, and some as pastors and teachers, for the equipping of the saints for the work of service, to the building up of the body of Christ; until we all attain to the unity of the faith, and of the knowledge of the Son of God, to a mature man, to the measure of the stature which belongs to the fullness of Christ."
—Ephesians 4:11-13

"...that is the Spirit of truth, whom the world cannot receive, because it does not see Him or know Him, but you know Him because He abides with you and will be in you."
—John 14:17

LESSON FOUR

Because Christians live in a largely unbelieving and often antagonistic world, God has provided us with the strength to stand for Him. Jesus promised that His Spirit would come *upon* us to give us *power* to live the Christian life, and *boldness* to be a witness for Him.

From the following Scriptures, what did Jesus teach His disciples about the coming *upon* of the Holy Spirit?

> *"...you will receive power when the Holy Spirit has come upon you; and you shall be My witnesses..."*
> —Acts 1:8

Luke 24:49 _____
_____

Acts 1:4-8 _____
_____

Acts 2 gives the account of the day of Pentecost. Describe the events below.

> *"...the promise is for you ..."*
> —Acts 2:39

vs. 3-13 _____
_____
_____

vs. 14-36 _____
_____
_____

vs. 37-41 _____
_____
_____

vs. 42-47 _____
_____
_____

DAY 6

THE MINISTRY OF THE SPIRIT

Just as Jesus Christ met the needs of His disciples during His earthly ministry, the Holy Spirit will minister to each yielded believer in very practical ways. In this section, we will learn that the ministry of Holy Spirit in our lives is to be our Comforter, Companion, Convicter and Counselor.

> *"As one whom his mother comforts, so I will comfort you..."*
> —Isaiah 66:13

● **COMFORTER:** *"...He shall give you another Comforter, that He may abide with you forever."* —John 14:16

The comfort that the Holy Spirit offers is dual. When we are hurting or needy He offers us the infinite tenderness of a mother. But He also empowers us with courage to withstand the trials and frustrations of life. The word *comfort* comes from the Latin word *fortis* from which we get the word *fortify*.

Write about a personal experience when you have known either the tender or the strengthening comfort of the Holy Spirit.

_____
_____
_____
_____

LESSON FOUR

"That He would grant you, according to the riches of His glory, to be strengthened with power through His Spirit in the inner man,"
—Ephesians 3:16

- **COMPANION:** *"...I am with you always, even to the end of the age."*
—Matthew 28:20

As Christians, we are never alone, however, the circumstances of our life often press upon us and cause us to feel very much alone. In these times, we can become extremely vulnerable to the attack of the enemy of our soul. We must draw near to God, believing the promise of His loving, caring presence with us. In times like this, we should go to God's Word and let His companionship meet our emotional needs.

Read the promise in James 4:8a. How will you respond to loneliness, depression or the attacks of the enemy in the future?

_____
_____
_____
_____

"...I will never leave you nor forsake you."
—Hebrews 13:5

- **CONVICTER:** *"And He, when He comes, will convict the world concerning sin."*
—John 16:8

Because the Spirit is *holy* He will reproduce His holiness in us. Holiness means *separated unto God*. Any thought or action in our life that is not holy grieves the indwelling Holy Spirit. He does not depart from us when this occurs, instead He convicts us or speaks to us through our conscience.

Our conscience is our inner judge, which warns us and lets us feel the Spirit's grief when we are contemplating or participating in sin. The Bible urges us to keep a clear conscience. If we learn to quickly respond with obedience and repentance to the Spirit's *nudging* He will keep us from sin.

Describe a time when you experienced the conviction of the Holy Spirit. Did you yield to that conviction?

_____
_____
_____
_____

"...their conscience bearing witness, and their thoughts alternately accusing or else defending them"
—Romans 2:15

THE HOLY SPIRIT | 41

LESSON FOUR

"...He will guide you into all truth..."
—John 16:13

"And your ears will hear a word behind you, 'This is the way, walk in it,' whenever you turn to the right or to the left."
—Isaiah 30:21

- **COUNSELOR:** *"...And His name will be called Wonderful Counselor..."* —Isaiah 9:6

God counsels us with His Word, through godly people and by the inward guidance of His Holy Spirit. As we spend time in God's presence, we will learn to hear His voice and to discern His will. Many Christians neglect to develop intimacy with God through daily devotions and continue to stumble through life, missing the guidance and counsel of the Holy Spirit.

◆ Do you need God's wisdom today for a particular situation? ❑ Yes ❑ No
Explain. _____
_____
_____

What promise does God give in James 1:5,6? _____
_____
_____
_____

> **FOUNDATION TRUTH:** *The Holy Spirit is our Comforter in all of our difficulties, our ever-present Companion, our Convicter in times of temptation, and our Counselor when we need guidance and wisdom.*

"The grace of the Lord Jesus Christ, and the love of God, and the fellowship of the Holy Spirit, be with you all."
—2 Corinthians 13:14

DAY 7

Go back through Lesson Four and review the four *Foundation Truths* that you learned. Write these truths below.

1) _____
_____
_____

2) _____
_____
_____

3) _____
_____
_____

4) _____
_____
_____

LESSON FIVE

SPIRITUAL GROWTH & MATURITY
DAY 1

The Bible describes the new believer as a *babe* in Christ. Just as a healthy baby experiences the various stages of growth before reaching mature adulthood, the baby Christian must steadily progress on the path to *spiritual* maturity. Our Heavenly Father desires all of His children to develop into mature men and women of faith.

It is tragic when a baby fails to grow and become a healthy, mature adult. It is likewise grievous when a Christian stops short of spiritual wholeness and maturity. In this lesson we will study the life of the apostle Paul as an example to us to press on to spiritual maturity.

PAUL'S SALVATION

Paul was a religious man from his youth, though he did not come to faith in Christ until much later in his life. Read the following Scriptures and write out what you learn about Paul's life.

Acts 22:3 _____
_____
_____

Acts 23:6 _____
_____
_____

Acts 26:4-5 _____
_____
_____

Galatians 1:14 _____
_____
_____

Paul's zeal for his Jewish religion and its laws were displayed most vividly in his persecution of the Christian church. He believed that persecuting Christ's followers was a service unto God so he did it with a clear conscience. Read the Scriptures below and summarize Paul's actions toward believers. (Note that prior to Paul's conversion to Christ he was called Saul.)

Acts 7:54-60; 8:1-3 _____
_____
_____

> "...like newborn babes, long for the pure milk of the word, that by it you may grow in respect to salvation."
> —1 Peter 2:2

> "Therefore leaving the elementary teaching about the Christ, let us press on to maturity..."
> —Hebrews 6:1

> "This is a true saying, and everyone should believe it: Christ Jesus came into the world to save sinners— and I was the worst of them all."
> —1 Timothy 1:15 (NLT)

SPIRITUAL GROWTH AND MATURITY | 43

LESSON FIVE

Acts 22:4; 22:19; 26:9-11 _____
_____
_____

Galatians 1:13-14 _____
_____
_____

Philippians 3:4-6 _____
_____
_____

Many agree that Paul's conversion to Christianity was one of the greatest and most important events in church history. Read the exciting account in Acts 9:1-22 and briefly rewrite the story in your own words.

_____
_____
_____
_____
_____

Though Paul had lived a deceived life, His encounter with Jesus Christ completely transformed him. Read his testimony in 1 Timothy 1:12-16 and write out some of the key points.

_____
_____
_____
_____
_____

> **FOUNDATION TRUTH:** *God does not choose us to be His children, or adopt us into His family because of any virtue of our own, but by His grace alone.*

PAUL'S SERVICE

As an instrument in God's hand, Paul was sent out by Him, impassioned and empowered by the Holy Spirit to accomplish great things.

> **Apostle** - *A messenger; one sent out on a mission, who derives his authority from the sender.*

PAUL'S WORK FOR THE LORD

◆ **Missionary and church planter** — The Lord sent Paul on three missionary journeys to areas where the gospel had not been previously preached. He estab-

---

"To me, the very least of all saints, this grace was given, to preach to the Gentiles the unfathomable riches of Christ,"
—Ephesians 3:8

"...he is a chosen instrument of Mine..."
—Acts 9:15

"...when they had fasted and prayed and laid their hands on them, they sent them away...being sent out by the Holy Spirit, they went..."
—Acts 13:3-4

lished many churches in these cities. Paul's missionary travels are recorded in Acts, Chapters 13-21.

◆ **Preacher and teacher** — As was foretold, Paul preached Christ to gentiles, kings and the sons of Israel. Many believed in Christ, while others mocked and persecuted him. Examples of Paul's sermons are recorded in Acts 13:16-41 and Acts 17:22-34.

◆ **Writer** — Of the 27 books forming the New Testament, Paul was the author of thirteen and possibly fourteen of them. These books were actually letters or epistles written to churches he had established on his missionary journeys.

From prideful religious leader and persecutor of God's people to humble servant of the Almighty God, Paul's life is an example to all believers. Though few lives follow such extremes, we all like Paul have gone from darkness to light, from pridefully defying God's truth to humbly receiving His gift of salvation by grace.

What wonderful promise does God give to all believers in Ephesians 2:10?
_____
_____

◆ Do you believe that God has a plan and purpose for your life? ❏ Yes ❏ No

FOUNDATION TRUTH: *Regardless of our past mistakes or failures, God's calling and purpose for every believer is to have a relationship with Him and to serve Him by serving others.*

DAY 2
SANCTIFICATION

The biblical term for the Christian's maturing process is *sanctification*.

Sanctification - *Separated or set apart unto and devoted to God. Separation from the practice of sin and all that displeases and is opposed to God.*

The word can also be translated *holy*. Holiness is neither a feeling nor an experience but a lifestyle in which the character of the Son of God is developed within us and lived out in our daily lives.

Read 1 Peter 1:15,16 and write out the verses below.
_____
_____
_____
_____

"...to bear My name before the Gentiles and kings and the sons of Israel."
—Acts 9:15b

"...we are bound to give thanks to God always for you, brethren beloved by the Lord, because God from the beginning chose you for salvation through sanctification by the Spirit and belief in the truth..."
—2 Thessalonians 2:13

LESSON FIVE

"By this will we have been sanctified through the offering of the body of Jesus Christ once for all."
—Hebrews 10:10

The process of sanctification has three major aspects; initial, progressive and ultimate sanctification.

● INITIAL SANCTIFICATION

Initial sanctification is what God does for every believer. This position bears no relationship to our behavior. At the moment of conversion He sanctifies or sets us apart unto Himself. All believers have been redeemed, cleansed, forgiven, justified and made righteous through the blood of Christ. If we are truly born again we are sanctified by God. The Bible calls us *saints*, not because we are faultless or sinless, but because Jesus took our guilt upon Himself on the cross and we are now blameless before God.

"I am speaking in human terms because of the weakness of your flesh. For just as you presented your members as slaves to impurity and to lawlessness, resulting in further lawlessness, so now present your members as slaves to righteousness, resulting in sanctification."
—Romans 6:19

● PROGRESSIVE SANCTIFICATION

Progressing in sanctification is entirely dependent upon the believer's daily decision to abide in Christ and receive His power. God desires us to willingly surrender our lives to Him, and in a sense sanctify *ourselves*. As we yield to Him and desire His will in our life we will progress in sanctification.

Every time we consciously offer or present ourselves to God, set our minds on things above and walk by the power of the Holy Spirit, we are separating ourselves unto God and therefore progressing in sanctification. This moment by moment victory should be ever increasing as we come to know our own helplessness and God's absolute power in our life.

"Now may the God of peace Himself sanctify you entirely; and may your spirit and soul and body be preserved complete, without blame at the coming of our Lord Jesus Christ"
—1 Thessalonians 5:23

● ULTIMATE SANCTIFICATION

This absolute and final sanctification will occur when we are fully conformed to the image of Jesus Christ at His coming. As long as we are in our earthly bodies, we retain a fallen nature that is prone to sin. However, someday we will be fully conformed to the image of Christ when we depart from this life and awaken in His presence.

The following illustration helps us understand the process of sanctification:

"...we shall be like Him..."
—1 John 3:2

> *An expert of fine brass was searching through a pile of junk on the outskirts of the city, when he suddenly spied an old, battered brass pot. It was dirty, stained and beaten up, but his practiced eye recognized a thing of value. He made his way through the junk and picked up the old pot and **set it apart** by itself. In so doing, he **sanctified** that vessel. This is **sanctification** in its initial application. Of course he must spend many hours **cleansing**, **straightening out the dents** and **polishing** the old pot, until it becomes a thing of beauty to grace his table. This process is **sanctification** in its second application.*

LESSON FIVE

Jesus Christ searched us out of the junk pile of this world. When we responded to Him with saving faith He set us apart for Himself. He is now committed to cleanse us, straighten out our *dents*, polish us and make us a thing of beauty for His glory. Jesus is faithful to complete the work He began in our life. Our part is to yield to Him daily. As we abide in Him and remain faithful to surrender to His will, we will feel His sanctifying hand in our life and experience all that He has for us.

In his letter to the Philippian church Paul wrote of his confidence in the Lord's faithfulness in the sanctification process. Read Philippians 1:6 and rewrite the verse below.

_____

> *"He brought me up out of the pit of destruction, out of the miry clay; and He set my feet upon a rock making my footsteps firm."*
> —Psalm 40:2

FOUNDATION TRUTH: *God sanctified us when we received Christ as Savior and Lord. He continues to sanctify us as we walk with Him in love and obedience. One day He will welcome us into His presence and, in that moment, our sanctification will be complete.*

DAY 3

PAUL'S SANCTIFICATION

Paul was saved and set apart for service by Jesus Christ. His heart's desire was to have fellowship with Christ, to make spiritual progress and to become more and more like Christ.

Turn in your Bible to Philippians 3 and read the entire chapter.

Why did Paul willingly suffer the loss of all things (verses 7 and 8)?

_____
_____

Though Paul *knew* Jesus Christ, what was his heart's desire (verse 10)?

_____
_____

> *"For my determined purpose is that I may know Him – that I may progressively become more deeply and intimately acquainted with Him, perceiving and recognizing and understanding the wonders of His Person more strongly and more clearly. And that I may in that same way come to know the power outflowing from His resurrection which it exerts over believers..."*
> —Philippians 3:10 (Amplified Bible)

> **Intimate** - *Marked by very close association, contact or familiarity. A warm friendship developing through long association. Suggesting informal warmth or privacy; of a very personal or private nature.*

In the Old Testament, Moses asked God to give him a deeper knowledge of Himself and His ways. Read Moses' prayer in Exodus 33:13.

◆ Do you think this is the kind of prayer that God answers? ❑ Yes ❑ No

> *"Now therefore, I pray you, if I have found favor in your sight, let me know your ways that I may know you, so that I may find favor in your sight. Consider too, that this nation is your people."*
> —Exodus 33:13

SPIRITUAL GROWTH AND MATURITY | 47

LESSON FIVE

How do we come to know a person intimately? _____
_____
_____
_____

◆ Is this the desire of your heart? ❑ Yes ❑ No

How do you think we can come to know God more intimately?
_____
_____
_____
_____

In Philippians 3:12-14, Paul confessed that he had not become fully mature. He then compared himself to an athlete running a race. He used three descriptive phrases to explain what he did in order to make spiritual progress. As believers, it is our part to,

Lay hold — *To obtain the prize with the idea of eager and strenuous exertion.*
Press on — *To pursue with earnestness and diligence in order to obtain.*
Reach forward — *Stretching for the finish line as in a race.*

"...So run your race that you may lay hold of the prize and make it yours."
—1 Corinthians 9:24 (Amplified Bible)

Paul's comparison of the Christian to an athlete pressing on, laying hold and reaching forward emphasizes the truth that spiritual maturity is the result of commitment and discipline. Salvation is free to all who will repent and receive Christ, however, maturity is a daily choice requiring effort and sacrifice. Just as a casual athlete cannot excel in his sport, a casual Christian will have minimal growth and transformation.

FOUNDATION TRUTH: *Spiritual growth and maturity requires commitment, endurance and personal effort.*

DAY 4

HINDRANCES TO SPIRITUAL GROWTH

Hinder - *To interfere with the progress of, encumber, hold back, impede, obstruct.*

A runner in a race will be hindered from running strong and finishing well if he **focuses behind from where he has come, on other runners,** or **on himself** rather than on the goal. Paul addresses these three dangers in Philippians, Chapter 3.

LESSON FIVE

● **THE DANGER OF LOOKING BACK**

According to Philippians 3:13, what one thing did Paul do? _____
_____

Based on what you have learned about Paul in this lesson, what events in his past do you think he needed to forget? _____
_____
_____

To forget in this sense does not mean to cease to remember, but to choose to put behind you. We must not allow past sins or hurtful memories to dominate the present and rob our future, but put them behind us and move forward in God's grace, forgiveness and power.

Turn in your Bible to 1 Corinthians 15:9-10. How does Paul describe himself and what Christ did for him? _____
_____
_____

Do you think Paul could have served the Lord as effectively if he had focused on his past failures and sin, rather than on the grace of God? ❏ Yes ❏ No

Explain: _____
_____

"For I am the least of the apostles, and not fit to be called an apostle, because I persecuted the church of God."
—1 Corinthians 15:9

Though Paul was ashamed of his past, he knew that his freedom from it was found in repentance before God and walking in His grace. He could then forget the past and go forward.

◆ Is there anything in your life that you believe is hindering you from running the race? ❏ Yes ❏ No

Explain: _____
_____
_____
_____

◆ Perhaps God has used this lesson to expose present circumstances or past memories that you need to commit to Him, and receive His guidance and healing in order to leave it behind you. If so, are you willing to open up and share with your discipler, accountability person or prayer partner? ❏ Yes ❏ No

Explain: _____
_____
_____

"The Lord will accomplish what concerns me; Thy lovingkindness, O Lord, is everlasting..."
—Psalm 138:8

SPIRITUAL GROWTH AND MATURITY | 49

LESSON FIVE

● THE DANGER OF FOCUSING ON OTHERS

How did Paul describe some of the people in his life in Philippians 3:2,18,19?
_____
_____
_____

Read 2 Timothy 4:14-17 and describe Paul's experiences with others. How did he respond to them? _____
_____
_____

In Acts 7:54-60 we read that Paul was present when Stephen was being stoned to death. Undoubtedly his witness made a lasting impression on Paul. How did Stephen respond to his persecutors.
_____
_____
_____

◆ Do you think this scene influenced Paul's attitude toward those who would later persecute, offend or hurt him?   ❏ Yes   ❏ No

Explain: _____
_____

Paul forgave the offenses that others committed against him. For further insight into these offenses read 2 Corinthians 11:23-33. How much did Paul have to forgive? _____
_____

When teaching His disciples to pray, Jesus instructed them on the importance of forgiveness. Summarize what you learn in Matthew 6:9-15. (Note that forgiveness is not dependent upon the offender's worthiness to be forgiven.)
_____
_____
_____

Jesus also taught about forgiveness in a parable in Matthew 18:21-35. Read the parable and summarize its meaning. (It is important to note that this parable is not about salvation, for salvation is absolutely an issue of grace and is a gift from God given unconditionally, even though we have our part to do in accepting this free gift.)
_____
_____
_____

"Then Peter came to Him and said, "Lord, how often shall my brother sin against me, and I forgive him? Up to seven times?" Jesus said to him, "I do not say to you, up to seven times, but up to seventy times seven."
—Matthew 18:21, 22

LESSON FIVE

The Bible teaches that an offense against another is like a *debt* owed. The one who is offended can either forgive the debt or demand payment. However, the consequence of unforgiveness is bitterness, which poisons the heart. As sinners we owe God an enormous debt that we cannot pay. When we receive Christ as our Savior our debt is graciously forgiven, the penalty for that debt being placed on Christ.

God continues to forgive us daily. He *commands* us to forgive those who have offended us. Turn to Luke 6:35 and write the verse below. _____
_____

"See to it that no one comes short of the grace of God; that no root of bitterness springing up causes trouble, and by it many be defiled."
—Hebrews 12:15

◆ Is it possible that your spiritual growth been hindered because you have been focusing on others or failed to forgive?   ❏ Yes   ❏ No

Explain: _____
_____

Lesson Six, *Biblical Principles of Forgiveness and Reconciliation*, offers an in-depth study on the subject.

● THE DANGER OF FOCUSING ON OURSELVES

Though Paul was a man who did many things which he would later regret, he also had the potential for confidence in his own accomplishments.

Read Philippians 3:3-6 and write below what you believe Paul is expressing.
_____
_____

As a Jew, Paul believed that he was a good, even a righteous man. In Philippians 3:6 he states that he was blameless according to the standard of his old life and religion. When he met Christ, he understood the reality of his fallen condition and ceased putting confidence in himself or in his own goodness.

"A man's pride will bring him low, but a humble spirit will obtain honor."
—Proverbs 29:23

Self-confidence — *Putting faith or trust in ourself and our own abilities.*

The biblical term for self-confidence is pride.

Pride — *To congratulate oneself because of something one is, has, or has done or achieved. Conceit, haughtiness or arrogance.*

According to Proverbs 16:18, what will always be the result of pride? _____
_____
_____

"For all that is in the world, the lust of the flesh and the lust of the eyes and the boastful pride of life, is not from the Father, but is from the world."
—I John 2:16

SPIRITUAL GROWTH AND MATURITY | 51

LESSON FIVE

Pride exalts self and denies the need for absolute dependence upon God.

The dangers of focusing on self are many; self-centeredness, self-service, self-conceit, self-deceit, self-indulgence, self-seeking, self-reliance, selfishness and ultimately self-worship.

Read James 3:13-16. What do you learn about selfish ambition from these verses?
_____
_____
_____

According to Luke 9:23,24, what does Jesus say every believer must do?
_____
_____

What do you think it means to deny yourself? _____
_____
_____

FOUNDATION TRUTH: *To make spiritual progress, we must keep our focus on the goal of intimacy with Christ and spiritual maturity.*

"...let us strip off and throw aside every encumbrance – unnecessary weight – and that sin which so readily (deftly and cleverly) clings to and entangles us, and let us run with patient endurance and steady and active persistence the appointed course of the race that is set before us."
—Hebrews 12:1 (Amplified Bible)

DAY 5
THE WEIGHT OF SIN

Just as a runner in a race knows he will run faster and endure longer if he doesn't carry excess weight, Christians must constantly be aware of the *hindrance* of the excess weight of sin in their lives. Sin hinders us from making spiritual progress because it distracts us from our goal of spiritual maturity, separates us from fellowship and intimacy with our Heavenly Father and quenches the power of the Holy Spirit in our lives.

How does Romans 14:23b define sin? _____
_____

"...your iniquities have made a separation between you and your God, and your sins have hidden His face from you so that He does not hear."
—Isaiah 59:2

God has made provision for us to *strip off* and *throw aside* the entanglements of sin, and be restored to a right relationship with Him, through *reconciliation*.

Reconciliation — *To restore to friendship or harmony.*

- **THE STEPS TO RECONCILIATION WITH GOD**

Step 1: Confess — *To admit, own or acknowledge, to say the same.*

To confess our sins is to agree with God that our actions have truly been in opposition to His will and ways. What God calls sin is sin.

LESSON FIVE

"If we confess our sins, He is faithful and righteous to forgive us our sins and to cleanse us from all unrighteousness."
1 John 1:9

Step 2: Repent — *To be sorry, to change one's mind, to turn from sin.*

To request God's forgiveness is our response to being broken, sorry, and repentant that our actions have been against Him and have separated us from fellowship with Him.

"Look upon my affliction and my trouble, and forgive all my sins."
Psalm 25:18

Step 3: Believe and Receive

When we have obeyed Step 1 and 2, we must follow with the final step of believing and receiving. Based upon God's faithfulness and His Word, we accept His forgiveness, confident that our fellowship with Him will be restored.

"And all things you ask in prayer, believing you will receive."
Matthew 21:22

> *"If the Spirit of God detects anything in you that is wrong, He does not ask you to put it right; He asks you to accept the light, and He will put it right. A child of the light confesses instantly and stands bared before God; a child of darkness says – "Oh, I can explain that away." When once the light breaks and the conviction of wrong comes, be a child of the light, and confess, and God will deal with what is wrong; if you vindicate yourself, you prove yourself to be a child of the darkness."*
> —Oswald Chambers

Because we are weak in and of ourselves, we will regularly fail to live by God's standard of holiness. We will fall short of absolute love, kindness, patience, and forgiveness toward others. We have a natural *bend* towards selfishness; the potential to offend and be easily offended, to think more of ourselves and less of others, and to judgmentally hold the people in our lives to a standard that we ourselves cannot attain. Therefore, we must practice these steps daily!

When we have offended or sinned against another person, what does the Bible tell us that we should do? Read Matthew 5:23,24 for the answer. _____
_____
_____

FOUNDATION TRUTH: As unnecessary weight slows a runner's pace, sin in our life hinders our spiritual progress.

DAY 6

THE BELIEVER'S GOAL

Throughout chapter 3 of Philippians Paul weaves the theme of his personal goal and the purpose for his life and existence. In verse 14 he characterized this goal

"I press on toward the goal for the prize of the upward call of God in Christ Jesus."
—Philippians 3:14

LESSON FIVE

and purpose as the *"upward call of God in Christ Jesus."* This *upward call* can be summed up in two words, Christ and Heaven.

As you read the following verses that describe Paul's goal, allow the Lord to speak to you about your own life. Consider your own personal goals and the purpose for your life and existence and write your thoughts below each verse.

> *"He (the runner) sets the goal and the goal governs his entire existence."*
> —Michael Johnson, Olympic Runner

● KNOWING CHRIST
"...progressively becoming more deeply and intimately acquainted with Him, of perceiving and recognizing and understanding Him more fully and clearly..." v.8 (Amplified Bible)

_____
_____

● BEING FOUND IN CHRIST
"And that I may actually be found and known as in Him, not having any self-achieved righteousness that can be called my own...but possessing that genuine righteousness which comes through faith in Christ..." v. 9 (Amplified Bible)

_____
_____

● KNOWING CHRIST'S POWER
"For my determined purpose is that I may know Him - that I may progressively become more deeply and intimately acquainted with Him, perceiving and recognizing and understanding the wonders of His person more strongly and more clearly. And that I may in that same way come to know the power outflowing from His resurrection which it exerts over believers..." v. 10 (Amplified Bible)

_____
_____
_____
_____

● BECOMING LIKE CHRIST
"...that I may so share His sufferings as to be continually transformed in spirit into His likeness..." v.10 (Amplified Bible)

_____
_____
_____

● HEAVEN
Read Philippians 3:11, 20-21. Write out the main points below.

_____
_____
_____
_____

● INVENTORY OF YOUR PERSONAL GOALS

◆ Do you have a desire to grow in your intimate relationship with Christ?
  ❑ Yes ❑ No

◆ Do you want to become more like Christ in your daily life and actions?
  ❑ Yes ❑ No

◆ Is spiritual growth and maturity your personal goal?
  ❑ Yes ❑ No

◆ Are you willing to...

  ...forget the hurts or wrongs in your past, ceasing to let them effect the present and your future?
  ❑ Yes ❑ No

  ...forgive those who have failed, offended or hurt you?
  ❑ Yes ❑ No

  ...deny yourself and daily submit to Christ as Lord of your life?
  ❑ Yes ❑ No

  ...address the sin issue in your life by confessing and repenting of any known sin and believing and receiving God's forgiveness and restored fellowship?
  ❑ Yes ❑ No

What has God shown you that you need to do to *"press on toward the goal"*?

_____
_____
_____
_____

Paul was willing to expose his very heart to his readers. He confessed and gave an account of his faults and weaknesses, and boldly proclaimed his love for Christ and his passion for holiness and spiritual maturity. His life story is recorded for our encouragement and as an example for us to follow.

◆ Are you, like Paul willing to be open, accountable and even vulnerable to others in order to make spiritual progress?   ❑ Yes ❑ No

  Accountability — *Subject to giving an account, answerable, a statement explaining one's conduct.*

If you don't already have an accountability person or prayer partner in your life, contact your pastor or other church leader and express your desire for this type of encouragement and accountability.

"Confess your faults one to another, and pray one for another, that ye may be healed. The effectual fervent prayer of a righteous man availeth much."
—James 5:16
(King James Version)

LESSON FIVE

DAY 7

Go back through Lesson Five and review the six *Foundation Truths* that you learned. Rewrite these truths below.

1) _____
_____
_____

2) _____
_____
_____

3) _____
_____
_____

4) _____
_____
_____

5) _____
_____
_____

6) _____
_____
_____

LESSON SIX

FORGIVENESS & RECONCILIATION

DAY 1

THE COST OF UNFORGIVENESS

The word *forgive* means literally, *to give away*. When a debt is forgiven, the rights to payment are *given away*. If someone injures us and we forgive them, we *give away* the freedom to continue being angry and resentful towards the one who wronged us. We absorb the loss ourselves. The word *pardon* is derived from the Latin word, *perdonare*, meaning to *grant freely*. True forgiveness is undeserved, unmerited and free. It is not *just* or *fair*. In the Scriptures, to *forget* means, *to let go from one's power*.

When we refuse to grant forgiveness, choosing rather to maintain our *right* to demand payment for wrongs done to us, we also must be willing to absorb the cost incurred by that choice. Forgiveness is free, however unforgiveness is costly. Unwillingness to forgive results in *resentment*. Resentment, which means *to feel again*, clings to the past, reliving it over and over. Like *picking a scab*, resentment prohibits our wounds from healing.

"See to it that no one comes short of the grace of God; that no root of bitterness springing up causes trouble, and by it many be defiled."
—Hebrews 12:15

In Hebrews 12:15 we learn that bitterness, like a deep root, takes a firm hold in the human heart, then grows, and produces *fruit*. However, rather than nourish others, this fruit is bitter, causes trouble and defiles others.

Most of us do not readily admit that we have been harboring unforgiveness. However, Ephesians 4:31 teaches that there is undeniable evidence in an individual's life that the bitter root of resentment is growing within their heart.

Wrath – *An outburst of a strong, vengeful anger or indignation, seeking retribution.*

Anger – *A state of mind marked by fretfulness and grief.*

"Let all bitterness and wrath and anger and clamor and slander be put away from you, along with all malice."
—Ephesians 4:31

Evil speaking – *Unkind words, verbal abuse against someone, slander, wounding someone's reputation by evil reports, backbiting, insult and defamation.*

Malice – *Hateful feelings that we nurture in our hearts. A desire to see another suffer.*

● **THE FRUIT OF UNFORGIVENESS**

Ask yourself if any of the following are evident in your life:

- Pride
- Self-righteousness
- Self-pity
- Lack of trust in relationships
- Lack of intimacy in marriage
- Sexual dysfunction

LESSON SIX

- Emotional instability
- Anxiety, tension & stress
- Health problems
- Eating disorders
- Judgmental & critical of others
- Ultra-sensitive & easily offended
- Absence of peace & joy
- Broken fellowship with Jesus

FOUNDATION TRUTH: *Unforgiveness results in bitterness, defiles other relationships and troubles the human heart.*

DAY 2

WHY FORGIVE?

Besides the before mentioned devastation that results from unforgiveness, we are to forgive because:

◆ **God commands it.**

"But love your enemies, and do good...and you will be sons of the Most High; for He Himself is kind to ungrateful and evil men. Be merciful, just as your Father is merciful."
—Luke 6:35,36

"And whenever you stand praying. If you have anything against anyone, forgive him, that your Father in heaven may also forgive you your trespasses."
—Mark 11:25

Obedience to our Heavenly Father is not optional. If we pick and choose when we will and will not obey God's commands, we will live unfruitful, ineffective and spiritually barren lives.

◆ **When we forgive others, we resemble Jesus and bear His likeness.**

"Then Jesus said, 'Father, forgive them, for they do not know what they do'."
—Luke 23:34

"the one who says he abides in Him ought to walk in the same manner as He walked."
—1 John 2:6

As Christians, we have the privilege and calling to carry the name of Christ to a lost world. In fact, the term *Christian* means *little Christ*. We must be willing to walk as He walked. Christ demonstrated forgiveness. He came to this earth to bring forgiveness to the guilty. He gave the commission to the church to continue proclaiming forgiveness. We must, if we are to rightly bear His name, forgive those who have offended us!

◆ **Forgiveness is the only means of breaking the cycle of blame and suffering.**

Forgiveness offers the way out and an end to strife! It does not and can not settle all questions of blame and fairness, but once forgiveness is extended such questions become irrelevant. It does allow a relationship to start over and begin anew.

LESSON SIX

This truth is demonstrated beautifully in the life of Joseph, recorded in Genesis chapters 37-45. Though he was misunderstood, mistreated, betrayed, abandoned by his brothers, and sold into slavery, he refused to allow the root of bitterness to take hold of his life. Shortly before being reunited with his brothers, he testified of the healing work that God had done in his life during the years of separation, as demonstrated in the naming of his sons. In Genesis 41:51,52 we read:

> *"Joseph named the firstborn Manasseh, 'For,' he said, 'God has made me forget all my trouble in all my father's household.' "*

> *"He named the second Ephraim, 'For,' he said, 'God has made me fruitful in the land of my affliction...' "*

To *forget* in this sense does not mean to cease to remember, but *to let go*, to cease to let the memory of hurtful things control your present life. Joseph's *fruitfulness* was directly related to his *forgetfulness*. Remember that resentment means *to feel again.* Joseph chose to trust God with his feelings, emotions and his past.

◆ **Unforgiveness imprisons us to the past and hinders the potential for a spiritually fruitful life.**

During Joseph's years alone in Egypt he allowed God to heal his heart, which had been broken by his own brothers and circumstances. Later, when given the opportunity, Joseph extended love, forgiveness and grace to his brothers. Joseph speaks to them in Genesis 45:

"Now do not be grieved or angry with yourselves, because you sold me here, for God sent me before you to preserve life...and to keep you alive by a great deliverance...He kissed all his brothers and wept on them, and afterward his brothers talked with him."

There was no blaming, no explanations demanded, only the voice of mercy and forgiveness. The way was cleared for Joseph and his brothers to be reunited and begin a new relationship.

◆ **Forgiveness relieves the burden of guilt in the offender.**

> *"When Joseph's brothers saw that their father was dead, they said, "What if Joseph bears a grudge against us and pays us back in full for all the wrong which we did to him!"...But Joseph said to them, "Do not be afraid, for am I in God's place?...So he comforted them and spoke kindly to them." Genesis 50:15-21*

Joseph's brothers would have carried their grief and guilt to their graves if he had not extended forgiveness to them. Forgiveness, undeserved and unearned, removed the guilt. If Jesus had not extended kindness to sinners, we would

"...in the ages to come He might show the surpassing riches of His grace in kindness toward us in Christ Jesus."
—Ephesians 2:7

FORGIVENESS AND RECONCILIATION

LESSON SIX

remain in the stranglehold of guilt. He made the first move toward us that made it possible for us to be reconciled to Him.

> **FOUNDATION TRUTH:** *God commands us to forgive and in doing so we bear the likeness of His Son and allow healing and reconciliation to begin.*

DAY 3

GOD'S SOVEREIGNTY AND MAN'S SUFFERING

Sovereign — *Possessing supreme power, unlimited wisdom, and absolute authority.*

"All the inhabitants of the earth are accounted as nothing, but He does according to His will in the host of heaven and among the inhabitants of the earth; and no one can ward off His hand or say to Him 'What have You done?'"
—Daniel 4:35

> *"... You have searched me and known me. You know when I sit down and when I rise up; You understand my thought from afar. You scrutinize my path and my lying down, and are intimately acquainted with all my ways. Even before there is a word on my tongue, Behold, O Lord, You know it all."*
> —Psalm 139:1-4

Psalm 139:1-18 teaches that God knows us intimately. All of our days were fashioned and ordained by Him. Before you knew God, or accepted Him as Lord and Savior He foreknew you and foreordained all the days of your life. God also gave you the gift of freewill that you might follow Him, but also gave you the freedom to reject Him, and His perfect plan for your life.

Many ask the question, *"If God were sovereign and in control why do His children suffer?"* The answer is simple, but must be accepted with a heart of trust and faith toward God. As we saw in Lesson One, we live in a fallen world. God has given all mankind freedom to follow Him and do good, and freedom to reject Him and choose evil. Therefore, both believers and non-believers are affected by the evil choices of others. God has an eternal plan; good *will* prevail and all evil, suffering and sorrow will cease. Until that time, if God shielded His children from evil, allowing only good, the unsaved would only be motivated to turn to Him for the guarantee of an easy life. This is the very argument that began the historic showdown in heaven between God and Satan in the life of Job.

Satan said to God,

"Does Job fear God for nothing? Have You not made a hedge about him and his house and all that he has, on every side? You have blessed the work of his hands, and his possessions have increased in the land. But put forth Your hand now and touch all that he has; he will surely curse You to Your face."
—Job 1:9-11

LESSON SIX

God *allowed* Satan to bring evil upon Job through the loss of his possessions, his children, and finally his health. God is a loving Father and does not *bring* evil into our lives, however for His purpose and for our ultimate good, He *allows* us to be touched by evil. The outcome of Job's suffering was trust, greater faith and intimacy with God.

Job did not understand *why* God was *allowing* him to suffer (God had declared in Job 2:3 that Job was a righteous man), therefore he asked God, "W*hy?*" For several chapters Job agonizes over this question, seeking a satisfactory answer. God never answers the question, instead He directs Job's attention to His power and glory, which are displayed in His creation. Job is satisfied with a newfound understanding of the greatness of God.

When we suffer we, like Job, want an explanation. *"Why, why, why?"* One of the many lessons we learn from Job is that *"Why?"* is the wrong question. We should instead ask God, *"What?"* *"What are You trying to teach me? What is Your will for me in this season of suffering?"*

◆ Knowing that God is sovereign, is there a part of your life that is beyond His power, wisdom, or authority?   ❏ Yes ❏ No

◆ Is there a day or a circumstance that has touched you that God did not know beforehand?   ❏ Yes ❏ No

◆ How should you respond to life's disappointments, difficulties, suffering, and trials? _____
_____
_____
_____

We can choose to harbor bitterness toward others; parents who failed us, a spouse who deserted us, friends who disappointed us, a drunk driver who killed a loved-one, and so forth, or we can place our faith in a sovereign God and forgive the offenses and failures of others.

When we accept Christ as Savior and Lord, we put our trust in Him for our eternal destiny. We must also trust Him with our past experiences and our present circumstances. He alone can comfort us in and through our trials and strengthen us to do the right thing. He alone can bring good out of bad and restore relationships that have been broken. Our obedience to God's Word will give us peace and bring praise, honor, and glory to our Lord Jesus Christ.

FOUNDATION TRUTH: *God has the perfect plan for our life with all the details of His plan laid out before us. Our responsibility is to ask "What is Your plan?"*

"...God cannot be tempted by evil, and He Himself does not tempt anyone..."
—James 1:13

"Then Job answered the Lord and said, 'I know that You can do all things, and that no purpose of Yours can be thwarted... I have heard of You by the hearing of the ear; but now my eye sees You...'"
—Job 42:1-5

"Have I sinned? What have I done to you, O watcher of men? Why have you set me as your target, so that I am a burden to myself?"
—Job 7:20

"Why do you hide Your face and consider me Your enemy?"
—Job 13:24

FORGIVENESS AND RECONCILIATION

LESSON SIX

"...In this you greatly rejoice, even though now for a little while, if necessary, you have been distressed by various trials, so that the proof of your faith, being more precious than gold which is perishable, even though tested by fire, may be found to result in praise and glory and honor at the revelation of Jesus Christ."
—1 Peter 1:6-7

DAY 4

TRIALS AND TRIBULATION

Jesus taught His followers that trials and tribulations are part of the life of a disciple.

> *"...In the world you have tribulation, but take courage; I have overcome the world."*
> —John 16:33

Tribulation - *Pressure, affliction, anguish, burden, persecution and trouble.*

Just as the refiner places the crude gold into the crucible and turns up the heat in order to bring the dross to the surface, God places His beloved children in the crucible of suffering in order to both refine us and transform us into the image of Christ.

> *"He will sit as a smelter and purifier of silver, and He will purify the sons of Levi and refine them like gold and silver, so that they may present to the Lord offerings in righteousness."*
> —Malachi 3:3

If we trust Him in this process our lives will permeate with the love, hope and confidence of Jesus Christ. As others look at us, they will see Christ in us.

> *"And we know that all things work together for good to those who love God, to those who are the called according to His purpose. For whom He foreknew, He also predestined to become conformed to the image of His Son..."*
> —Romans 8:28-29

This verse does not say *some things*, but *all things*. The key is faith. If we choose to believe God's promises and trust Him in the midst of our trials and tribulations we will be victorious and God will be glorified in our life.

◆ Are you willing to:

Allow God to transform your life through your trials?
❑ Yes ❑ No

Trust God with the pain that others may have caused in your life?
❑ Yes ❑ No

Obey God and forgive others in order to be set free from the bondage and pain that has resulted from unforgiveness in your life?
❑ Yes ❑ No

"These things I have spoken to you, that in Me you may have peace. In the world you will have tribulation' but be of good cheer, I have overcome the world."
—John 16:33

LESSON SIX

What has God revealed to you personally in the area of forgiveness? How will you obey Him? _____
_____
_____

"There are times, says Jesus, when God cannot lift the darkness from you, but trust Him. God will appear like an unkind friend, but He is not; He will appear like an unnatural Father, but He is not; He will appear like an unjust judge, but He is not. Keep the notion of the mind of God behind all things strong and growing. Nothing happens in any particular situation unless God's will is behind it, therefore you can rest in perfect confidence in Him."
—Oswald Chambers

FOUNDATION TRUTH: *God's Word tells us that God will use our trials and tribulations to transform us into His image.*

RECONCILIATION

To *reconcile* means to restore to friendship or harmony, or to settle or resolve differences. It is the doing away with enmity, and the bridging over of a quarrel. Reconciliation implies that the parties being reconciled were formerly hostile to one another. Because God loved the world and desired to reconcile man to Himself, He sent His Son to die in our behalf. The blood of Christ is the means of doing away with enmity between man and God. Through Christ, we are reconciled to God. It is in God's character to restore what has been broken. He desires to reconcile or restore us to one another.

The Scriptures instruct us in Ephesians 4:31-32 to *"Let all bitterness…be put away from you…be kind…tenderhearted, forgiving…"*

- How do we put away bitterness?
- How do we reconcile with someone who we have offended?
- How do we repair the hurt we have caused others?
- How do we forgive someone who has offended us?
- How can we change our own feelings about a wrong done?

DAY 5

IF YOU NEED TO BE FORGIVEN

If you have been wrong, offended or hurt another, as an act of the will you must,

Step 1 — Confess your sin to God and ask Him to forgive you and to fill your heart with His love.

"And through Him to reconcile all things to Himself, having made peace through the blood of His cross; through Him, I say whether things on earth or things in heaven. And although you were formerly alienated and hostile in mind, engaged in evil deeds, yet He has now reconciled you in His fleshly body through death, in order to present you before Him holy and blameless and beyond reproach."
—Colossians 1:20-22

"For if while we were enemies we were reconciled to God through the death of His Son, much more, having been reconciled, we shall be saved by His life."
—Romans 5:10

LESSON SIX

"If we confess our sins, He is faithful and just to forgive us our sins and to cleanse us from all unrighteousness."
—1 John 1:9

"As far as the east is from the west, so far has He removed our transgressions from us."
—Psalm 103:12

"Therefore if you bring your gift to the altar, and there remember that your brother has something against you, leave your gift there before the altar, and go your way. First be reconciled to your brother, and then come and offer your gift."
—Matthew 5:23-24

"But seek first the kingdom of God and His righteousness, and all these things shall be added to you."
—Matthew 6:33

"Blessed is he whose transgression is forgiven, whose sin is covered...When I kept silent, my bones grew old through my groaning all the day long. For day and night Your hand was heavy upon me; my vitality was turned into the drought of summer. I acknowledged my sin to You and my iniquity I have not hidden. I said, "I will confess my transgressions to the Lord," and You forgave the iniquity of my sin."
—Psalm 32:1,3-5

Take a moment right now to cry out to God, asking Him to forgive you and to fill you with His Holy Spirit to strengthen you to obey. God alone forgives sins. He forgives and He forgets. By faith, accept God's absolute forgiveness and cleansing.

Step 2 — If possible, go to those you have offended, confess your wrong actions or attitude, and ask for their forgiveness.

> Six of the most powerful words
> in the English language,
> **"I was wrong. Please forgive me."**

Read Matthew 5:23-24 and write out your commitment to obey.

_____
_____
_____
_____

If possible, do this face to face. However, due to distance, you may have to communicate with the person by telephone or in writing. Don't let distractions or other obstacles delay this act of obedience.

Go to a trustworthy Christian friend, your discipler, accountability person or prayer partner and share with them what the Lord is doing in your life in this important area of forgiveness. Ask them to prayer partner with you and hold you accountable to follow through on your commitment.

Step 3 — Spend time daily with the Lord in His Word and in prayer.

We develop an intimate relationship with the Savior and receive His wisdom and power through spending time with Him daily, allowing Him to speak to us in His Word and respond back to Him in prayer. Write out your decision to the Lord to spend time with Him daily in prayer, reading of His Word and meditation.

_____
_____
_____

Step 4 — Ponder the meaning of the cross and the sacrifice Jesus made for your sins.

Take a moment right now and thank Jesus for all that He has done for you, for forgiving you for all of your sins, for His perfect plan of transforming you into His image through this trial, and for the gift of His Holy Spirit.

> **FOUNDATION TRUTH:** God's Word commands us to go to any we have offended and humbly ask forgiveness.

IF YOU NEED TO FORGIVE

If another person has wronged, offended or hurt you, as an act of the will you must,

Step 1 — Pray and ask God for the strength to obey and forgive the person or persons.

God promised to give us the strength to move mountains. This may be your Mt. Everest! We know that it is God's will that we forgive others, so we can be confident that if we ask for His strength, it will be granted.

> "Whenever I see myself before God and realize something of what my blessed Lord has done for me at Calvary, I am ready to forgive anybody anything, I cannot withhold it. I do not even want to withhold it.
> —Dr. Martyn Lloyd-Jones

Step 2 — Communicate your forgiveness to the person or persons.

The word *forgive* is a *verb*, or an *action word*. To truly forgive requires you to *take action*. God is using His Word to speak to you right now, revealing truth for you to obey and *act upon*.

Read Jesus' parable on forgiveness in Matthew 18:21-35. Describe the two very different responses of the lord of the slave and the slave from verses 27 and 28?

_____
_____
_____

Release — *To free fully, to relieve or dismiss.*
Seize — *To retain or keep hold on.*
Choke — *To throttle, strangle or drown.*

According to verses 34 and 35, what did the lord of the slave do in response to the slave's unwillingness to forgive? _____
_____
_____

LESSON SIX

"For we ourselves were also once foolish, disobedient, deceived, serving various lusts and pleasures, living in malice and envy, hateful and hating one another. But when the kindness and the love of God our Savior toward man appeared, not by works of righteousness which we have done, but according to His mercy He saved us, through the washing of regeneration and renewing of the Holy Spirit."
—Titus 3:3-5

"Now this is the confidence that we have in Him, that if we ask anything according to His will, He hears us."
—1 John 5:14

*"And the lord of that slave felt compassion and **released** him and forgave him the debt. But that slave went out and found one of his fellow slaves who owed him a hundred denarii; and he **seized** him and began to **choke** him saying, 'Pay back what you owe.'"*
—Matthew 18:27-28

LESSON SIX

"For if you forgive men their trespasses, your Heavenly Father will also forgive you."
—Matthew 6:14

Note: *This Scripture is not teaching that a born again child of God will experience eternal ruin if unwilling to forgive. It does state that they will be imprisoned by their unforgiveness. See 1 Corinthians 11:30-32 and* The Fruit of Unforgiveness *from Day 1 of this lesson.*

Forgiveness is not an easy thing to do, therefore you must not try to stand alone, but seek the support and accountability of a mature Christian friend, spouse, or prayer partner.

> *"Forgiveness is not an emotion...Forgiveness is an act of the will, and the will can function regardless of the temperature of the heart."*
> —Corrie ten Boom

Write out your commitment to forgive the person or persons, and give yourself a date to contact them by, so you won't let yourself put it off!

_____
_____
_____
_____

- Do I have to go to them in person?
- Can I call or write them instead?

In some cases, due to distance, cost of travel, safety to you, or the ability of the other person to be quiet long enough to let you say what you need to say, a letter, email or telephone call may be the best way for you to accomplish this.

Keep these points in mind when speaking or communicating in writing,

◆ **You are doing this out of obedience to your Heavenly Father who loves and cares for you.**

He wants you to be free from the bondage and oppression you have been experiencing as a result of unforgiveness.

◆ **You do not have to rehearse every detail or act of the offense against you.**

Many times, especially when forgiving parents, they are completely unaware of what they may have done that hurt you. In other cases, it may have been blatant sin against you, for example, sexual, physical, or emotional abuse, rape, abandonment by a parent, friend, or spouse, slander spoken against you, etc. In these cases, you can be more specific as to why you need to forgive.

"The degree to which I am able and willing to forgive others is a clear indication of the extent to which I have personally experienced my Heavenly Father's forgiveness for me."
—Phillip Keller

◆ **Do not try to compel others to own up to their offenses.**

God has called you to obey, not to be a prosecuting attorney, jury or judge! Keep it short. In most cases, due to the high level of emotions, we can find ourselves saying things we did not plan on saying that may undermine the purpose of the meeting, letter, or conversation.

- **Finally, ask them to forgive you for harboring bitterness toward them.**

Remember that what they may have done was wrong and offensive, but bitterness and unforgiveness is equally wrong.

> **FOUNDATION TRUTH:** God's Word commands believers to humbly forgive others who have offended or wronged them.

DAY 6
MAINTAINING YOUR COMMITMENT TO FORGIVE

The person you have forgiven may continue to be a regular part of your life; possibly a parent, a child or a spouse. When this is the case you may encounter a spiritual battle after you have asked for forgiveness or forgiven them.

The forgiveness experience has changed you, but it has not necessarily changed *them*. God has had a major victory in your life in bringing you to this place of surrender and obedience, however, their position may not have changed! They may continue to hold onto bitterness toward you. If this is the case you need to seek God *daily* for His strength to extend mercy and compassion to them, without compromising.

If you forgave a parent for being harsh and unloving, and asked them to forgive you for harboring bitterness, yet the next time you see them, they continue to be harsh and unloving, your flesh may want to react in the way you formerly reacted.

God will be faithful to produce His fruit in your life as you surrender to Him moment by moment. You must keep in mind that your obedience in forgiving was not so that the other person or persons would change. Unless they surrender their lives and experiences to the Lord, they cannot change. Only God can change our hearts and renew our minds, and only if we surrender to Him.

Depending on the severity of your situation and the seriousness of the circumstances you may consider seeking godly counsel on appropriate and wise boundaries with the other person.

OUR SPIRITUAL BATTLE

As you will learn in Lesson Seven, we are involved in a spiritual battle every day. Satan, does not want you to obey God or have victory over sin, therefore, he

"But the fruit of the Spirit is love, joy, peace, longsuffering, kindness, goodness, faithfulness, gentleness, self-control. Against such there is no law. And those who are Christ's have crucified the flesh with its passions and desires. If we live in the Spirit, let us also walk in the Spirit. Let us not become conceited, provoking one another, envying one another."
—*Galatians 5:22-26*

"For we do not wrestle against flesh and blood, but against principalities, against powers, against the rulers of the darkness of this age, against spiritual hosts of wickedness in the heavenly places."
—*Ephesians 6:12*

LESSON SIX

"Be angry, and do not sin; do not let the sun go down on your wrath, nor give an opportunity to the devil."
—Ephesians 4:26,27

"Finally brethren, whatever things are true, whatever things are noble, whatever things are just, whatever things are pure, whatever things are lovely, whatever things are of good report, if there is any virtue and if there is anything praiseworthy – meditate on these things."
—Philippians 4:8

"Now may the God of hope fill you with all joy and peace in believing, that you may abound in hope by the power of the Holy Spirit."
—Romans 15:13

"Therefore humble yourselves under the mighty hand of God… casting all your care upon Him, for He cares for you…your adversary the devil walks about like a roaring lion, seeking whom he may devour. Resist him, steadfast in the faith…"
—1 Peter 5:6-9

will attack your mind with past memories, evil thoughts, lies, temptations, and condemnation. You must exercise self-control and remember what and whom you are battling!

This is the reality in which we live! Satan hates to lose ground in our lives. He does not like the idea that he has lost the ability to continue to rob us of God's peace and joy.

How do we stop giving the devil *opportunities* to work his destruction in our lives?

◆ **Take each thought that enters your mind and measure it by God's Word to see if it is from God, from your flesh, or from the enemy.**

According to 2 Corinthians 10:3-5 what should we do with each thought that enters our mind?_____
_____
_____

From Philippians 4:8, what kinds of thoughts should occupy our minds?
_____
_____
_____

◆ **Pray in each instant of decision for God's power to do His will.**

"Do not be overcome by evil, but overcome evil with good."
—Romans 12:21

You may have developed the habit of responding to an individual with anger, self-defense or other negative behavior. In order to break this habit and develop godly responses, you must be in fellowship with Christ, sensitive to the leading of the Holy Spirit and submitting to His will and ways.

◆ **Resist and rebuke the devil in the name of Jesus.**

"Yet Michael the archangel, in contending with the devil…dared not bring against him a reviling accusation, but said, "The Lord rebuke you!""
—Jude 1:9

God wants you to be aware of the devil's devices so that you can have victory. Unforgiveness is one of Satan's most powerful tactics to keep God's people in bondage!

LESSON SIX

What if the person that I am forgiving does not want to reconcile the relationship?

You must keep in mind that you are only responsible for your part of reconciliation. Regardless of the position the other person takes, you must obey God by asking for and giving forgiveness. If the other person refuses to grant you forgiveness or if they do not acknowledge their wrong toward you, God will still bless you for your obedience and pour out His peace, grace, and mercy upon your life. You will still experience His freedom from your bondage regardless of the other person's response.

You cannot place any expectations or requirements upon what the other person may say or do, but surrender all to the Lord and trust Him to work in the midst of your circumstances. This is a major inner personal battle that many people face with this act of obedience. We must not lean on our own understanding, but obey and surrender to God and His will.

God has given us spiritual laws to govern and protect us. His Word gives us understanding and instructions us how to follow these laws. Our flesh, pride and fear will keep us from trusting and obeying God in these situations, but through the power of the Holy Spirit we can overcome.

Pray this prayer,

"Lord Jesus, I pray for the strength to trust You in these circumstances. Help me to remember that I am doing this for You. I do not look to... for anything, but place my life in Your hands. I pray for reconciliation with ..., but I know that I can only do my part. I pray for...to surrender to You that You might be glorified. I trust you entirely with the results. In Jesus Name I pray. Amen"

What if the person I need to forgive is deceased? Can I still forgive them?

Bitterness in the human heart lives on long after the object of that bitterness has died. Forgiveness is not optional, but a requirement from God which His children must obey. The death of the offender does not nullify God's Word. True, biblical forgiveness requires us to take action. We must do more than agree in our minds or hearts that we should forgive. The Bible does not command us to merely feel forgiveness. We must exercise our will and follow through with our actions!

You must begin by confessing your bitterness for the deceased person to the Lord. To *confess* means to *acknowledge or disclose one's misdeed, fault or sin.* Then tell the Lord that you are no longer holding their faults or offenses against them, but forgiving. It is helpful to speak your confession out loud and verbalize your forgiveness in the presence of a trusted friend, spouse, pastor, counselor, etc.

"Trust in the Lord with all your heart, and lean not on your own understanding; in all your ways acknowledge Him and He shall direct your paths."
—Proverbs 3:5-6

LESSON SIX

Use the following prayer to help guide you:

"Lord Jesus, thank you for dying on the cross and forgiving me for all of my sins. I agree with Your Word that I must forgive this person for the hurt they caused me. I ask You for the strength to obey and speak these words of forgiveness.

I forgive...for...(you may need to be specific). I ask you to take away my bitterness and forgive me for holding onto this bitterness for so long. In Jesus Name I pray. Amen"

FOUNDATION TRUTH: God's Word tells us to continue in obedience to Him regardless of the responses or actions of others.

DAY 7
CONCLUSION

It is awfully hard to forgive. It is harder *not* to forgive. If we do not forgive, we deny what Jesus has done for us on the cross (see Matthew 6:14-15). Our experience of God's forgiveness is directly related to our ability to forgive. A readiness to forgive others is part of the indication that we have truly repented and received God's forgiveness. A broken heart toward God cannot be a hard heart toward others.

Pride and fear keep us from forgiveness and reconciliation. Refusing to give in, or be broken, insisting on our rights, and defending ourselves are all indications that our selfish pride is ruling our life, rather than the Lord. If fears of 'what-ifs' are consuming and controlling you, you need to pray for the faith to trust and obey God. Enemies are very expensive to keep. Matthew 18:21-35 warns that an unforgiving heart will put us in an emotional prison.

Go back through Lesson Six and review the seven **Foundation Truths** that you learned. Rewrite these truths below.

1) _____
_____
_____

2) _____
_____
_____

> *"The first and often the only person to be healed by forgiveness is the person who does the forgiving... When we genuinely forgive, we set a prisoner free and then discover that the prisoner we set free was us."*
> —Lewis Smedes

LESSON SIX

3) _____
   _____
   _____

4) _____
   _____
   _____

5) _____
   _____
   _____

6) _____
   _____
   _____

7) _____
   _____
   _____

LESSON SEVEN

"The truth is that, although we lead normal human lives, the battle we are fighting is on the spiritual level. The very weapons we use are not human but powerful in God's warfare for the destruction of the enemy's strongholds."
—2 Corinthians 10:3-4 (Phillips Translation)

SPIRITUAL WARFARE

It is very important that we understand that as believers we are engaged in a battle, a *spiritual* battle. Everyday this battle rages on around us and within our very souls. We must choose to stand and fight in the victory that Christ has secured for us, or be defeated!

In this lesson you will learn why you are in a spiritual battle, and how to identify your enemies and have victory in the battle. In addition, you will also learn how to be strong in your Christian walk and to overcome in your personal war against sin.

DAY 1
SETTING THE STAGE

In Lesson Two we studied Genesis 2 and 3 and learned about the Garden of Eden and the perfect environment that God provided for man. Satan, embodied in the snake entered the scene and shrewdly deceived the woman from trusting and obeying the Lord. As a result Adam and Eve did not trust and obey the Lord.

Man had been given authority over the earth (Genesis 1:28-31), and a garden to cultivate and keep (Genesis 2:15). When Adam and Eve sinned, the entire human race, Satan, and the world were impacted. What resulted was the spiritual warfare that we continue to experience today. In the following section we will study the condition of the world, Satan and mankind as a result of sin entering the world.

THE WORLD AFTER THE FALL

As a result of the fall of man, this world now lies in the power of the devil. Evidence of this truth is all around us. Read the following verses about the condition of this world.

John 12:31 _____
_____
_____

1 Corinthians 11:32 _____
_____
_____

2 Peter 2:20 _____
_____
_____

LESSON SEVEN

1 John 5:19 _____
_____
_____

SATAN'S CONDITION AFTER THE FALL

When man fell into sin, he surrendered dominion of the earth to Satan. What do you learn about Satan from the following Scriptures?

John 14:30, John 16:11_____
_____
_____

2 Corinthians 4:4 _____
_____
_____

Ephesians 2:2 _____
_____
_____

MAN'S CONDITION AFTER THE FALL

Man was originally created in God's likeness. Bearing God's image, Adam was undefiled and eternal. After Adam's fall whose likeness did the subsequent generations bear according to Genesis 5:1-3?
_____

How do the following Scriptures describe the human race? Note the use of the words *all* and *none* in these verses.

Psalms 14:1-3 _____
_____

Isaiah 53:6 _____
_____

Romans 3:10-18 _____
_____
_____

Jesus affirms that all who do not have faith in Him continue to be lead by the devil's influence. Who, according to Jesus, is the father of all non-believers? Read John 8:38,41,44 for the answer. _____
_____

SPIRITUAL WARFARE | 73

Read 2 Timothy 2:25-26. By whom are all non-believers held captive?

_____

> **FOUNDATION TRUTH:** *God's entire creation was defiled when Adam and Eve sinned in the Garden of Eden. Satan continues to pursue man in an attempt to persuade him to deny his Creator.*

DAY 2

THE ENEMIES OF MAN | THE WORLD, THE FLESH & THE DEVIL

"For our struggle is not against flesh and blood, but against the rulers, against the powers, against the world forces of this darkness, against the spiritual forces of wickedness in the heavenly places."
—Ephesians 6:12

Most of us imagine that our enemy is someone who has offended or hurt us, therefore, we tend to focus on defending ourselves or contending with others; whether a driver who cut us off on the freeway or an estranged family member. However, the Bible teaches that our enemies are not other people, and that our struggles are actually *spiritual*. Our enemies are the world, our own flesh and the devil.

THE ENEMIES OF MAN — THE WORLD

As we saw in the previous section, this world is now Satan's domain. The systems of this world, such as politics, economics, education, fashion, entertainment, and the philosophies of man are under his evil influence. But Satan's dominion is only temporary. This is God's world and He will reclaim it for Himself.

When Jesus became a man, He brought God's kingdom to the earth. Turn in your Bible to Luke 17:20,21. What did Jesus say to the Pharisees, the Jewish religious leaders? _____

_____

"For the wisdom of this world is foolishness ..."
—1 Corinthians 3:19

When we are born again we become members of God's kingdom. Read Philippians 3:20 and Colossians 1:13 and write what you learn from these verses.

_____

_____

_____

"For God so loved the world that He gave His only begotten Son, that whoever believes in Him should not perish but have everlasting life. For God did not send His Son into the world to condemn the world, but that the world through Him might be saved."
—John 3:16, 17

Though we are citizens of God's kingdom, we continue to live physically in this world, which is temporarily Satan's kingdom. We live in the midst of two opposing kingdoms.

Shortly before Jesus' arrest and crucifixion, He told His followers that the unbelieving world would hate them. Turn in your Bible to John 15:18-21 and 1 John 3:13 and comment on what you learn.

_____

_____

_____

Turn in your Bible to Colossians 2:8. What warning does this verse give? How do you believe this verse applies to you personally?
_____
_____

Read the Parable of the Sower in Mark 4:1-20. What are the three things that Satan uses to choke the Word of God from our hearts? _____
_____
_____

Satan is a poor loser! If he cannot possess a man's soul, he will be relentless to possess his affections, hold his attention, or distract him from the Kingdom of God to the trivial things of this world. God instructs us with three warnings for living in this world. Look up the following verses and fill in the blanks.

Romans 12:1-2 _____
_____

James 4:4 _____
_____

1 John 2:15 _____
_____

FOUNDATION TRUTH: *God is asking His children to voluntarily refuse to identify with this world, and to live according to the principles of His kingdom.*

DAY 3

THE ENEMIES OF MAN | THE FLESH

Our flesh is our old sin nature; the habits, desires, thoughts and reactions from our life prior to surrendering to Christ. The flesh is our old *self,* or as Scripture says, our *old man.* The flesh wants to get its own way, cares only about itself, and does not want to live according to God's standards or will. In one sense, Christians have two opposing natures dwelling within – the spirit and the flesh!

What do you learn about the battle of our spirit and our flesh in Galatians 5:17?
_____
_____

Read Romans 6 and answer the following questions.

What died with Christ? (vs. 2-11) _____

LESSON SEVEN

"For whatever is born of God overcomes the world ; and this is the victory that has overcome the world — our faith."
—1 John 5:4

"Knowing this, that our old man is crucified with him, that the body of sin might be destroyed, that henceforth we should not serve sin."
—Romans 6:6

LESSON SEVEN

"For the flesh lusts against the Spirit, and the Spirit against the flesh; and these are contrary to one another, so that you do not do the things that you wish."
—Galatians 5:17

"...the flesh is weak"
—Mark 14:38

What did our old self die to and from what are we now freed?
(vs. 2, 6, 7, 10, 11)_____

What does God instruct us to do in our struggle against sin and our sin nature?
(vs. 13, 16, 19)_____
_____

Romans 6 teaches us that before coming to Christ, we were slaves to sin. What must we be enslaved to now in order to have victory over sin?
(vs. 16-18, 19, 22) _____
_____

Jesus atoned for *all* of our sins on the cross. Our sin nature *was* crucified and buried with Christ. As we claim this truth and, in obedience, continually present ourselves to God and abide in Him daily, we are freed from the power of sin!

Read Galatians 2:20 and rewrite the verse in your own words.

_____
_____
_____

DAY 4

THE ENEMIES OF MAN | THE DEVIL

Who is Satan? How does he work? Where did he come from? What is his final destination?

"How you are fallen from heaven, O Lucifer, son of the morning!"
—Isaiah 14:12

Many humorously imagine that the devil is a figure in a red spandex suit, holding a pitchfork, enticing us to do wrong. In reality the devil is the epitome of evil. All of the hurt and suffering of mankind has its origin in Satan. He is the enemy of God and God's children.

He is *not* the counterpart to God. He is powerful, but does not possess *all* power. He is cunning, but does not have *all* wisdom. He is able to wreak mass destruction, yet he himself *will* be destroyed.

"You were the anointed cherub who covers..."
—Ezekiel 28:14

Turn in your Bible and read Isaiah 14:12-17 and Ezekiel 28:12-19. These Scriptures give us background into who Satan is, how he works, where he came from and his fate.

Satan was originally a beautiful cherub or angel. His heart became lifted up with pride because of his beauty and he rebelled against God. In Isaiah 14, we read that five times he proclaimed, "I will." He wanted to rule heaven, the angels, the earth and the world. He said, "I will make myself like the Most High." He wanted to be God.

LESSON SEVEN

What was the immediate result of Satan's rebellion? (See Ezekiel 28:16-17 and Luke 10:18) _____
_____

When Satan was cast from heaven, the Bible suggests that he took one-third of the angels with him in his rebellion (2 Peter 2:4 and Revelations 12:4). These fallen angels or demons form Satan's army. In the Old Testament book of Daniel we learn that the demonic angels struggle against God's angels for control of nations, kingdoms and individuals (Daniel 10:13-21). According to Matthew 25:41 and Revelations 20:10, what is Satan's ultimate destiny? _____
_____

Knowing that he will one day be destroyed, Satan relentlessly pursues his course of destruction, blinding the minds of unbelievers (2 Corinthians 4:4) and contending with God's children. Look up the following verses and briefly comment on what you learn about his tactics.

Matthew 13:19 and Luke 8:12 _____
_____

2 Corinthians 2:11 _____
_____

2 Corinthians 11:14 _____
_____

1 Timothy 3:7 and 2 Timothy 2:26 _____
_____

Satan is very powerful, wise, organized and relentless in his attacks upon believers and non-believers. Man is no match for Satan. The devil is wiser and stronger than we are in our *own* wisdom and strength. However, God has provided for us to have absolute victory in Satan's attacks. We need not be defeated, deceived, or destroyed by our enemy. What do you learn about our victory over Satan's attacks following verses?

1 Peter 5:8 _____
_____

James 4:6-10 _____
_____

"...greater is He who is in you than he who is in the world."
—1 John 4:4

FOUNDATION TRUTH: *As believers in Christ, we have three formidable foes, which we must always be on guard against; this world system, our fallen nature of ungodly desires and the devil.*

LESSON SEVEN

"But thanks be to God, who gives us the victory through our Lord Jesus Christ."
—1Corinthians 15:57

"With all prayer and petition pray at all times in the Spirit, and with this in view, be on the alert with all perseverance and petition for all the saints."
—Ephesians 6:18

"Now to Him who is able to keep you from stumbling, and to make you stand in the presence of His glory blameless with great joy."
—Jude 1:24

DAY 5

VICTORY IN THE BATTLE

In this section, we will focus on Ephesians 6:10-18. Read these verses through several times before answering the following questions.

Where does spiritual strength come from? (v. 10) _____

How are we able to stand firm against the devil's schemes? (v. 11)
_____

THE ARMOR OF GOD

This spiritual armor has six components. Just as a soldier does not go to battle unless he is fully covered and armed, we must take up the full armor to stand firm in the strength of the Lord. It is important to note that most of the armor relates to the Word of God. Fill in the blanks below describing this full armor.

Loins girded with _____   Breastplate of _____
Shod feet with _____   Shield of _____
Helmet of _____   At all times _____
Sword of _____

Once the armor is in place, the believer is exhorted to **all** prayer at **all** times with **all** perseverance for **all** the saints. On every occasion and in all seasons we must have intimacy with our Heavenly Father through prayer.

As believers, living for Christ in a fallen world, we will continue to experience spiritual warfare. However, God has promised that we can stand firm in His victory and not be defeated by Satan. God will be faithful to keep us from falling and to deliver us safely to His presence in our heavenly home.

Read Psalm 13:4 What will happen if we neglect to take up God's provision?
_____
_____

> **FOUNDATION TRUTH:** God has guaranteed His children absolute victory in our spiritual battles, as we walk in the complete armor He has provided.

SATAN'S FLAMING ARROWS

Ephesians 6:16 teaches that the evil one attacks Christians with flaming arrows. Before we study the nature of these arrows, let's first seek understanding through the Scriptures about the tactics Satan uses in these attacks.

LESSON SEVEN

What word is used in Genesis 3:1 to describe Satan? _____

Crafty - *Wily, insidious, cunning or guile, with exceptional shrewdness.*

Ephesians 6:11 tells us to put on the full armor of God in order to stand firm against what? _____
_____
_____

Schemes - *Trickery, strategy, methodical, art, skill or cunning.*

What will Satan attempt to do, using his crafty scheming? See 2 Corinthians 11:3.
_____
_____
_____

According to 2 Corinthians 11:14, why do we not always recognize that we are under Satanic attack? _____
_____
_____

The following commentary on 2 Corinthians 11:14 from *Barnes' Notes* accurately describes spiritual warfare and Satan's offensive:

> "...Satan does not carry on an open warfare. He does not meet the Christian soldier face to face. He advances covertly; makes his approaches in darkness; employs cunning rather than power, and seeks rather to delude and betray than to vanquish by mere force...Satan does not openly appear. He approaches us not in repulsive forms, but comes to...lay before us some temptation that shall not immediately repel us. He presents the world in an alluring aspect; invites us to pleasures that seem to be harmless, and leads us in indulgence until we have gone so far that we cannot retreat."

Satan's arrows are aimed at our mind (thought life and will) and our heart (the center of our emotions). Our enemy knows that if he can control our thoughts and feelings, he can then influence our behavior. What do the following verses state about our minds and heart?

Proverbs 23:7 _____
_____
_____

Proverbs 4:23 _____
_____
_____

SPIRITUAL WARFARE

LESSON SEVEN

How did Satan attack in the following verses?

Matthew 16:21-23 _____
_____
_____
_____

John 13:2 _____
_____
_____
_____

Acts 5:3 _____
_____
_____
_____

> "...the devil...does not stand in the truth because there is no truth in him...he is a liar and the father of lies."
> —John 8:44

> "And the tempter came ..."
> —Matthew 4:3

> "... the accuser of our brethren has been thrown down, he who accuses them before our God day and night."
> —Revelation 12:10

Satan is liar and deceiver (John 8:44), a tempter (Matthew 4:3, and an accuser (Revelation 12:10). His spiritual arsenal, therefore, consist of,

- **LIES**
- **TEMPTATIONS TO SIN**
- **CONDEMNATION**

Because our enemy is cunning and knows our weaknesses we must be careful to guard our heart and mind from his attacks. God Word tells us exactly how we must do this.

GUARDING YOUR HEART AND MIND

What do you learn from the following Scriptures about guarding your heart and mind from Satanic attacks?

2 Corinthians 10:3-6 _____
_____
_____
_____

Philippians 4:6-8 _____
_____
_____
_____

Isaiah 26:3 _____
_____
_____
_____

> "He who begins, finishes. He who leads us on, follows behind to deal in love with our poor attempts... He gathers up the things that we have dropped — our fallen resolutions, our mistakes...He makes His blessed pardon to flow over our sins till they are utterly washed away. And He turns to flight the enemy, who would pursue after us, to destroy us from behind."
> —Amy Carmichael

LESSON SEVEN

Hebrews 4:12 _____
_____
_____

Jesus was tempted by the devil, as recorded in Matthew 4:1-11. Read these verses through several times. With each flaming missile from the devil, Jesus responded with the words, *it is written*. What does this teach you about victory in spiritual warfare? _____
_____
_____
_____

What did the devil do in verse 11 as a result of Jesus confronting him with the truth of the Word of God? _____
_____
_____

Read the instruction and promise in James 4:7 and rewrite the verse.
_____
_____
_____

Read Ephesians 4:26,27. How do you believe we give the devil an opportunity?
_____
_____
_____

DAY 6
WHY CHRISTIANS CONTINUE TO SIN

As Christians, spiritual warfare is a part of our life on this earth, but as we have seen, we can have victory in Christ. Since this is true, why do believers continue to sin? The key to this struggle and overcoming the pull of sin in our life is found in understanding what the Bible calls *the desires of the flesh*.

Our natural desires were given to us by God and, of themselves, are not sinful. We feel hunger and thirst, so we satisfy that desire with food and drink. We feel tired, so we sleep. Sex is a normal desire; and blessed by God when fulfilled within the biblical guidelines of marriage. The fulfillment of these and other desires only become sinful when we seek to satisfy ourselves outside of the will of God.

The epistle of James provides straightforward teaching on how man's desires can lead to sinful behavior. Read James 1:13-17. According to verse 14, what is the true source of our temptation to sin? _____
_____

"...let us lay aside every weight, and the sin which so easily ensnares us, and let us run with endurance the race that is set before us, looking unto Jesus, the author and finisher of our faith..."
—Hebrews 12:1, 2

SPIRITUAL WARFARE | 81

LESSON SEVEN

> Sin will:
> Take you farther than you wanted to go,
> Keep you longer than you wanted to stay,
> Cost you more than you wanted to pay!

"The righteousness of the upright will deliver them, but the unfaithful will be caught by their lust."
—Proverbs 11:6

"We must acknowledge that there is such a thing as "the pleasures of sin" — temptation would not be so strong if this were not true. The answer is to make our love of God stronger than all temptation, and in that way to lead the Christian life."
—Peter Marshall, Sr.

"I am the vine, you are the branches; he who abides in Me and I in him, he bears much fruit, for apart from Me you can do nothing.
—John 15:5

To lust means to have an intense desire for something. We can lust in a positive sense. For example, lusting after God, which Jesus taught in the Sermon on the Mount.

> *"Blessed are those who hunger and thirst for righteousness, for they shall be satisfied."*
> —Matthew 5:6

James is not referring to lusting after godliness, but selfish craving. Satan knows our weaknesses and is ready to entice us with temptations to fulfill ourselves outside of the will of God.

Read James 1:15 and answer the following questions.

What happens when we give into the lusts of our flesh? _____
_____
_____

What does sin bring forth? _____

Though sin does not always cause physical death, the very nature of sin is to injure, harm and kill. Sin results in the death of honor, respect, trust, morals, innocence, dreams and goals. Marriages are broken, innocent children are devastated and lives are shattered when individuals, refusing God's way, choose instead to fulfill themselves apart from Him.

In our battle against the lusts of our own flesh, what are we instructed to do in 2 Timothy 2:22? _____
_____
_____

Those who do not know Christ are enslaved to sin, but the child of God has been set free from the grip of sin. Turn in your Bible to Galatians 5:16. What must we do in order to have victory over the lusts of our flesh? _____
_____
_____

ABIDING IN CHRIST AND WALKING IN THE SPIRIT

Victory over our flesh and the pull of sin is only possible when we determine moment by moment to abide in an intimate relationship with Christ and walk in the Spirit. This relationship with God does not just happen, but is a continual act of our will, choosing to offer our body, mind, will and emotions to God. We must admit and acknowledge our own depravity; that we are hopeless and helpless without Him, and depend upon Him with the assurance that He will be faithful to receive and strengthen us.

LESSON SEVEN

In Romans 8 we learn that abiding in Christ and walking in the Spirit means:

- Surrendering our minds (thoughts) to God's Spirit (verses 4-8)
- Putting to death the deeds of our flesh and fleshly desires (verse 13)
- Being led by God's Spirit (verse 14)
- Living in the freedom and blessings of being God's child (verses 15-17)
- Being helped in our weaknesses (verse 26)
- Living for God's purposes, rather than our own (verse 28)
- Being conformed to the image of Jesus (verses 29-30)
- Being freely given all things from God (verse 32)
- Being free from condemnation (verses 33-34)
- Experiencing a love relationship with Jesus Christ (verses 35-39)
- Having victory in our trials (verses 35-39)

FOUNDATION TRUTH: *As we abide in an intimate relationship with Christ and walk in the Spirit, we will have victory over our flesh and sin.*

◆ Have you been experiencing God's victory over the world, the flesh and the devil? ❑ Yes ❑ No
Explain: _____
_____
_____
_____
_____

How has God spoken to you in this chapter about your battle with sin?
_____
_____
_____
_____
_____
_____

What promises will you claim or instructions will you obey as a result of this lesson? _____
_____
_____
_____
_____
_____

> *"I can do all things through Him who strengthens me."*
> —Philippians 4:13

> *"What is more consistent with faith than to acknowledge ourselves naked of all virtue, that we may be clothed by God; empty of all good, that we may be filled by Him, slaves to sin that we may be liberated by Him; blind that we may be enlightened by Him; lame that we may be guided; weak that we may be supported by Him; to divest ourselves of all ground of glory, that He alone may be eminently glorious, and that we may glory in Him"*
> —John Calvin

LESSON SEVEN

DAY 7

Go back through Lesson Seven and review the five *Foundation Truths* that you learned. Rewrite these truths below.

1) _____
_____
_____

2) _____
_____
_____

3) _____
_____
_____

4) _____
_____
_____

5) _____
_____
_____

LESSON EIGHT

END TIMES

Man has always been both intrigued and fearful of the unknown. The *end of the world* is the popular theme of many motion pictures today. Television talk shows often leave viewers spellbound with guests giving graphic accounts of their spiritual journeys or *New Age* experiences. Best-selling books have been written giving testimonies of those who claim to have died and then returned to tell their story. Even the current popularity of angels confirms man's interest in what lies beyond this life.

Unfortunately, many speaking out today are not speaking reality and truth, but delusion. Some suggest that God is a *bright light* and that we need not fear death, because we will be embraced by this *light* when we pass from this life. As Christians, we must be careful and discerning so as not to become deceived.
But, how can we know or discern truth from error?

DAY 1

God's Word is the strong foundation upon which all truth stands. Jesus Christ proclaimed Himself to be the only way, the only truth and the only life. In John 14:6 Jesus said *"...no man comes to the Father but through Me."* Jesus stated in John 10:9 that He was the door, *"...if anyone enters through Me, he shall be saved..."* The test of truth from error is Jesus Christ.

◆ Is the life, death and resurrection of Jesus Christ being proclaimed?

◆ Is confession of sin, surrendering to Christ and obedience to His teaching being promoted?

Turn in your Bible to Galatians 1:6-9. Use the space below to rewrite the warning contained in these verses. _____
_____
_____

What is the truth about our eternal destiny? What happens when we die? What will heaven be like? In this final lesson, we will answer these questions and explore the biblical teaching about the end times. This will include death, the rapture of the church, the tribulation, the second coming of Jesus Christ, the resurrection, the millennial reign of Christ, the judgements, hell and the believer's eternal heavenly home!

The Bible, written thousands of years ago foretold the events that are now coming to pass. Read the following passages that describe the world situation during the end times.

> *"Beloved, do not believe every spirit, but test the spirits to see whether they are from God; because many false prophets have gone out into the world. By this you know the Spirit of God; every spirit that confesses that Jesus Christ has come in the flesh is from God; and every spirit that does not confess Jesus is not from God...."*
> —1 John 4:1-3

> *"For many deceivers have gone out into the world, those who do not acknowledge Jesus Christ...Watch yourselves...Anyone who goes too far and does not abide in the teachings of Christ, does not have God..."*
> —2 John 7-9

END TIMES | 85

LESSON EIGHT

"... you shall know the truth and the truth shall set you free."
—John 8:32

Daniel 12:4 _____
_____
_____

Matthew 24:1-14 _____
_____
_____

1 Timothy 4:1,2 _____
_____
_____

And because lawlessness will abound, the love of many will grow cold.
—Matthew 24:12

2 Timothy 3:1-7 _____
_____
_____
_____

These events have always occurred but their frequency and intensity will build as the earth prepares for the second coming of Christ. The Bible likens the end times activities to a woman in labor. The contractions become stronger and closer together as the time approaches to give birth.

THE DEATH OF THE BELIEVER

Death is a fearful fact of life. In fact, in Job 18:14 death is called *"the king of terrors"*. God has instilled within each of us the will to survive. As believers in Jesus Christ, we need not live this life fearing death or hopelessly grieving over saved loved ones who have passed away, but should be diligent to share the good news of Jesus Christ with those who are perishing without the knowledge of the Savior. Read the following Scriptures and write what you learn about the death of the believer.

"O Death, where is your sting? O Hades, where is your victory?"
—1 Corinthians 15:55

Hebrews 2:14,15 _____
_____
_____

1 Thessalonians 4:13 _____
_____
_____

"...our Lord Jesus Christ, ...has begotten us ...to an inheritance incorruptible and undefiled and that does not fade away, reserved in heaven for you..."
—1 Peter 1:3, 4

Psalm 116:15 _____
_____
_____

Proverbs 14:32 _____

86 | A STRONG FOUNDATION

LESSON EIGHT

THE BOSOM OF ABRAHAM

Before the death and resurrection of Jesus Christ, all men who died went to *Sheol* or *Hades*. Sheol was located in the heart of the earth and was divided into two compartments, separated by an impassable gulf. One part was called *Abraham's bosom*, where all those men and women of faith went to be comforted by Abraham when they died.

The other part of Sheol was the *abode of the wicked*, where unbelievers were sent when they died. Read the story that Jesus taught about Lazarus and the rich man in Luke 16:19-31 and write out the main points below.

_____
_____
_____

When Jesus was crucified He descended into Hades, emptied it of the righteous and ushered them to Paradise. Read the following verses and write out what you learned.

Matthew 12:40 _____
_____
_____

Ephesians 4:8-10 _____
_____
_____

Today when the righteous die they are immediately taken to Paradise, into the presence of Jesus Christ. In Paradise, God's children are both conscious and comforted by Jesus Christ. Paul was given a vision of Paradise as recorded in 2 Corinthians 12:4. The unrighteous continue to go to Hades to await the resurrection and final judgement. Read the Scriptures below and answer each question.

What did the Lord say to the thief on the cross in Luke 23:43?
_____
_____

What was Paul's desire? Philippians 1:21-23 _____
_____
_____

What was Paul's confidence? 2 Corinthians 5:1-8 _____
_____
_____

> *Therefore He says: "When He ascended on high, he led captivity captive, and gave gifts to men." (Now this, "He ascended"—what does it mean but that He also first descended into the lower parts of the earth? He who descended is also the One who ascended far above all the heavens, that He might fill all things.)*
> —Ephesians 4:8-10

> *"...death is only a passage out of a prison into a palace; out of a sea of troubles into a haven of rest; out of a crowd of enemies into the company of true, loving, and faithful friends; out of shame, bad feelings, and humiliation, into great and eternal glory."*
> —John Bunyan

END TIMES | 87

LESSON EIGHT

Read the account of the martyrdom of Stephen in Acts 7:54-60. What did he cry out in verse 59? _____

> **FOUNDATION TRUTH:** When Christians pass from this life, they are immediately ushered into the presence of Jesus in Paradise.

DAY 2
THE RAPTURE OF THE CHURCH

"Watch therefore, for you do not know what hour your Lord is coming."
—Matthew 24:42

The *rapture* refers to the event when Jesus Christ will snatch His church out of this world. The phrase *caught up* is found in 1 Thessalonians 4:17. It is the Greek word *harpazo*, which means to be *snatched away*. The Latin equivalent is the word *rapio*, where we get the word rapture. Turn in your Bible to the following Scriptures and write the key points.

1 Thessalonians 4:13-18 _____
_____
_____
_____

1 Corinthians 15:49-58 _____
_____
_____
_____

Matthew 24:36-44 _____
_____
_____
_____

1 Thessalonians 5:1-11 _____
_____
_____
_____

"Beloved, now we are children of God, and it has not appeared as yet what we shall be. We know that, when He appears, we shall be like Him, because we shall see Him just as He is."
—1 John 3:2

God's Word teaches that at the rapture of the church Jesus Christ will descend from heaven with a shout, with the voice of an archangel and with a trumpet blast. What a day that will be! The believers who have died and been in God's presence in paradise, will be resurrected and, together with living Christians, will be transformed *"in the twinkling of an eye"* and receive glorified bodies patterned after Christ's own resurrected body. Our earthly bodies, made of the dust of the earth are temporary. Our heavenly bodies will be eternal, suited for eternal life in heaven.

LESSON EIGHT

What will our glorified heavenly bodies be like? Will we have actual physical bodies? The answers to these questions are found as we read about the body of Jesus after His resurrection. Turn in your Bible to Luke 24:31, 36-43 and John 20:19-29 and use the space below to describe what you learn.

_____
_____
_____

FOUNDATION TRUTH: *Believers will receive their perfected, heavenly bodies at the rapture of the church.*

THE GREAT TRIBULATION

According to Job 5:7, *"Man is born unto trouble, as the sparks fly upward."* Jesus warned His disciples in John 16:33, *"in the world you shall have tribulation."* An undeniable and inescapable reality of life is the presence of problems, trials, and tribulation. We all experience minor irritations and disappointments, and sometimes, major hurts and sorrows. However, the great tribulation is a specific seven-year period in which God pours forth His wrath and judgement upon an unbelieving world.

"...as in the days of Noah..."
—Matthew 24:37, 38

In the days of Noah, God removed the righteous before bringing judgement and wrath upon the earth with the flood. Likewise, before God again brings mass judgement upon the earth with the great tribulation, He will graciously remove the righteous at the rapture. How do the following Scriptures comfort you as a believer regarding God's wrath to come during the great tribulation?

Romans 5:9 _____
_____
_____

1 Thessalonians 1:9,10 _____
_____
_____

1 Thessalonians 5:9 _____
_____
_____

What do you learn about the tribulation from Matthew 24:21, 22?
_____
_____
_____
_____
_____

"For then there will be great tribulation, such as has not been since the beginning of the world until this time, no, nor ever shall be. And unless those days were shortened, no flesh would be saved; but for the elect's sake those days will be shortened."
—Matthew 24:21-22

LESSON EIGHT

THE BOOK OF REVELATION

The most graphic description of the end times, including the tribulation are found in the book of Revelation. Because Revelation is often difficult to understand, many Christians are hesitant to read this wonderful book of the Bible. What promise does God give in Revelation 1:3 and 22:7 to those who do read the book of Revelation? _____

_____

THE SIX SEALS

In Revelation 5:1 a scroll sealed with seven seals is introduced. As the chapter proceeds, the seven seals are broken one by one and the events of the great tribulation unfold. As each seal is broken, great catastrophes and demonstrations of God's wrath and power begin to be poured out upon and overtake the earth. Follow along in Chapter 6 of Revelation in your Bible.

1. The false Christ comes to conquer — verses 1-2
2. Peace is taken from the earth — verses 3-4
3. Famine — verses 5-6
4. Death by sword, famine, pestilence and wild beasts — verses 7-8
5. Christians converted during tribulation are martyred — verses 9-11
6. Terror and environmental disasters — verses 12-17

THE SEVEN TRUMPETS

The breaking of the seventh seal in Revelation 8:1 is followed by silence in heaven, then a series of seven trumpet sounds. As the angels sound forth the first six trumpets, the earth continues to experience the wrath of God until the seventh trumpet, which announces the coming reign of Christ. Follow along in your Bible in Revelation 8:2-9:21 and 11:15-19.

1. One-third of the earth burned up — 8:7
2. One-third of the sea becomes blood — 8:8-9
3. One-third of the rivers are made bitter — 8:10-11
4. The moon and one-third of the stars are darkened — 8:12-13
5. Tormenting creatures are released from the bottomless pit — 9:1-12
6. One-third of mankind is annihilated by an invading army — 9:13-21
7. Thunder, lightening, earthquake and hail storm — 11:15-19

"And it shall come to pass in that day that the LORD will thresh, from the channel of the River to the Brook of Egypt; and you will be gathered one by one, O you children of Israel. So it shall be in that day: the great trumpet will be blown; they will come, who are about to perish in the land of Assyria, and they who are outcasts in the land of Egypt, and shall worship the LORD in the holy mount at Jerusalem."
—Isaiah 27:12, 13

LESSON EIGHT

THE SIX BOWLS OF WRATH

At the blast of the last trumpet, another series of judgements is poured forth, described in Revelation 16 as *seven bowls* filled with the wrath of God.

1. Sores appear on those who bear the mark of the beast — verse 2
2. The sea becomes blood and all sea life is killed — verse 3
3. The rivers and springs of water become blood — verse 4
4. The sun scorched men with fire — verse 8
5. The kingdom of the beast became darkened — verse 10
6. The Euphrates dried up to prepare for the coming battle — verse 12
7. Lightening, thunder and a great earthquake — verses 17-18

"It is a terrifying thing to fall into the hands of the Living God."
—Hebrews 10:31

THE BATTLE OF ARMAGEDDON

As the sixth bowl of God's judgement is emptied, it ushers in the great battle of God, the battle of Armageddon (16:13-16). The kings of the earth and their armies will be gathered to battle for one last world war. With the modern development of atomic weapons, and their destructive possibilities, the potential for warfare to totally destroy mankind is very real. This war ends in the final return of Jesus Christ to this earth. The Lord will return to save mankind from absolute annihilation!

"For our God is a consuming fire."
—Hebrews 12:29

FOUNDATION TRUTH: *The tribulation is a seven-year period when God will pour forth His wrath upon those who have rejected His Son.*

DAY 3
THE HEAVENLY SCENE

While the world is experiencing the outpouring of God's wrath, the raptured church is in heaven with Jesus! Two great events are taking place in heaven; the judgement (*bema*) seat of Christ and the marriage supper of the Lamb.

THE JUDGEMENT SEAT OF CHRIST

Jesus Christ took the judgement for our sin on the cross. We are saved by grace through faith in Jesus. The judgement seat of Christ is not a judgement of condemnation. All believers will stand before Christ and be judged and awarded for their faithfulness and service. What do you learn about the judgement seat of Christ from the following Scriptures?

"...we shall all stand before the judgment seat of Christ."
—Romans 14:10

LESSON EIGHT

1 Corinthians 3:11-15 _____
_____
_____

1 Corinthians 4:5 _____
_____
_____

2 Corinthians 5:9-11 _____
_____
_____

Like the crowns awarded to contestants in the Olympic games, believers will be awarded crowns. Read the following references and list these crowns.

- 2 Timothy 4:7,8 — The Crown of _____
- James 1:12 — The Crown of _____
- 1 Peter 5:4 — The Crown of _____

Because of our love for Christ and awe in His presence, what will we, like the elders, do with our crowns?

Revelation 4:10-11 _____
_____
_____

THE MARRIAGE SUPPER OF THE LAMB

After the judgement seat of Christ, the entire body of Christ will sit down together with Christ and partake of a banquet, the marriage supper of the Lamb. Christ will finally be joined for eternity to His bride (the church).

Describe the supper below.

Revelation 19:6-9 _____
_____

Matthew 26:29 _____
_____

Luke 12:37 _____
_____

Luke 14:15 _____

THE SECOND COMING OF JESUS CHRIST

LESSON EIGHT

The second coming of Jesus Christ will be one of the most dramatic events of all time! Christ's first coming to earth was marked with lowliness; born in a stable in an obscure village to a poor virgin, and heralded by common shepherds. His second coming will be a full display of His awesome power and glory.

At the completion of the marriage supper of the Lamb, Christ, along with the church, will rise from the supper table, mount white horses, and return to the earth as the battle of Armageddon rages. Read Revelation 19:11-21 and describe the scene.

_____
_____
_____

Christ will come to the earth with His church to execute final judgement upon unrepentant mankind. Read the following exciting verses and write what you learn about the second coming of Christ.

Zechariah 14:1-4 _____
_____
_____

Matthew 24:27-31 _____
_____
_____

Acts 1:11 _____
_____
_____

Revelation 1:7 _____
_____
_____

> **FOUNDATION TRUTH:** After Christ gathers His Church to heaven at the rapture, the believers will be given rewards for faithful service, join Him in the marriage supper and accompany Him as He returns to the earth for His second coming.

"...Enoch, in the seventh generation from Adam, prophesied, saying, 'Behold, the Lord came with many thousands of His holy ones, to execute judgement upon all, and to convict all the ungodly of all their ungodly deeds which they have done in an ungodly way, and of all the harsh things which ungodly sinners have spoken against Him.'"
—Jude 14,15

DAY 4

THE MILLENNIAL REIGN OF CHRIST

The millennium will be the thousand-year period following the second coming of Christ. Satan will be bound. Christ will set up His kingdom upon the earth. The

LESSON EIGHT

"If we endure, we will also reign with Him..."
—2 Timothy 2:12

raptured saints, along with the tribulation saints (Revelation 6:9-11), will reign with Christ. Read the following verses and describe the millennium.

Isaiah 2:1-5 _____
_____
_____

Isaiah 11:5-10 _____
_____
_____

Revelation 20:1-6 _____
_____
_____

When the millennium is completed, Satan will be released one final time. Read Revelation 20:7-10 and describe these events:

_____
_____
_____

DAY 5

THE WHITE THRONE JUDGEMENT

Ironically, all paths *do* lead to God. *Every* man *will* stand before the Creator, either humbly clothed with the righteousness of Christ or naked, guilty and condemned.

God has assigned all judgement to Jesus Christ (John 5:22-30 and Acts 17:31). At the white throne judgement the unrepentant sinners from all ages will be resurrected to stand before the One whom they have rejected. This is the second resurrection. Read Revelation 20:11-15 and describe the scene.

_____
_____
_____

"... He is coming to judge the earth. He will judge the world in righteousness, and the peoples in His faithfulness."
—Psalm 96:13

Turn to Romans 3:19. At the judgement of God will the guilty challenge God's authority and boastfully plead their innocence? _____

According to Philippians 2:9-11 how will all mankind, the guilty and the righteous, respond? _____
_____

As they stand before the white throne of God, the unsaved will acknowledge the Lordship of Jesus Christ, unto their condemnation, not unto salvation.

HELL

Many people reject the biblical doctrine of hell and reason that because God is a God of love He would never send anybody to hell. God *is* a God of love but does not send anybody to hell. He provided a way of escape through the blood of His Son. Therefore, people choose hell for themselves by rejecting the Savior. See John 3:16-21.

What is God's heart toward man regarding hell and judgement? Read 1 Timothy 2:3-6 and 2 Peter 3:9 _____
_____
_____

Summarize what you learn in Psalm 7:8-12. _____
_____
_____

God is a righteous judge who has a *right* to judge! If sinners refuse to repent and receive forgiveness God will judge them. Jesus brought grace to man but also boldly taught the reality of hell. Read the summarize the following teachings of Christ.

Matthew 13:42,50 _____
_____
_____

Matthew 25:41,46 _____
_____
_____

Mark 16:16 _____
_____
_____

FOUNDATION TRUTH: Christ taught that whoever rejects Him will face condemnation and judgement.

DAY 6

A NEW HEAVEN AND A NEW EARTH

When Jesus was preparing His disciples for His ascension to heaven, He sought to stir up within them a longing for heaven. Read the following Scriptures and summarize Jesus' words.

> "...a new heaven and a new earth; for the first heaven and the first earth passed away, and there is no longer any sea."
> —Revelation 21:1

LESSON EIGHT

John 14:1-3 _____
_____
_____

John 16:22 _____
_____
_____

"Rejoice and be glad, for your reward in Heaven is great..."
—Matthew 5:12a

Heaven is the place of supreme happiness because it is our Father's house. He is the head of His house. Everything about heaven reflects His holiness and glory. As members of God's household in heaven, we will live eternally in absolute peace, security and fulfillment. Never again will we know fear, sorrow, suffering, loneliness or hardship.

THE GLORY OF HEAVEN

In God's word we get a glimpse into the things that our Father has prepared for us. As you read Revelation 21 and 22 let God minister to you, encourage you as He reveals heaven to you and stirs up within your heart a longing for the Father's house! Complete the spaces below, describing heaven.

"... things which eye has not seen and ear has not heard, and which have not entered the heart of man, all that God has prepared for those that love Him. For to us God revealed them through the Spirit..."
—1Corinthians 2:9,10

- Heaven is a place where God (21:3) _____
- God will (21:4) _____
- There will be no (21:4) _____
- God makes all things (21:5) _____
- The one who thirsts (21:6) _____
- He who overcomes will (21:7) _____
- Heaven is brilliant, like (21:11) _____
- The wall is made of (21:18-20) _____
- The 12 gates are made of (21:21) _____
- The streets are made of (21:21) _____
- The temple in heaven is (21:22) _____
- Heaven is illuminated by (21:23) _____
- The gates will never (21:25) _____
- The citizens are those who (21:27) _____
- In heaven, there is a river of (22:1) _____
- There a tree of (22:2) _____
- There is no (22:3) _____
- There is a (22:3) _____
- In heaven we will (22:3-5) _____

96 | A STRONG FOUNDATION

Though we long to go to heaven, it is very human and natural to have questions and concerns. Will I still be me when I get to heaven? Will I know and recognize my loved ones? Will I remember this life? Carefully read the following Scriptures which address these questions.

- In Luke 16:19-31, Lazarus and the rich man retained their identity.
- In Matthew 17:2-3 Moses and Elijah were recognizable as themselves when they appeared to Jesus, Peter, James and John on the Mount of Transfiguration.
- In Mark 16:9-14 the disciples recognized Jesus Christ after His resurrection.
- In Philippians 4:3 we learn that our names are recorded in the Book of Life, signifying our eternal individuality and identity.

FOUNDATION TRUTH: *Heaven is a wonderful place, which God is preparing for all believers, where we will finally enjoy absolute love, joy, peace, freedom, fulfillment, and a right relationship with God and others.*

DAY 7
CONCLUSION

We began these lessons by looking up to the heavens and pondering our God who is enthroned on high. He created all things and continues to sustain His creation. Two thousand years ago He visited this earth in order to redeem the lost. Jesus Christ, the Son of God provided salvation for man by shedding His blood on the cross. The Holy Spirit dwells in each believer, empowering us to live a sanctified life. Our Heavenly Father has prepared a home for us and someday He will welcome each of His children home. How should we, who have put our trust in Jesus Christ, respond to the goodness of God? In 2 Peter 3:3-18 we are challenged to consider both God's judgement, and our own conduct and behavior. Fill in the blanks below.

Verse 11 — *I should be conducting myself* _____
_____
_____

Verse 12-13 — *I ought to be looking for and hastening* _____
_____
_____

Verse 14 — *I must be diligent to be found* _____
_____
_____

"...To Him be the glory, both now and to the day of eternity. Amen."
—2 Peter 3:18

"He brought me out of the pit of destruction, out of the miry clay, and He set my feet upon a rock making my footsteps firm."
—Psalm 40:2

LESSON EIGHT

Verse 17 — *I need to be on guard against* _____
_____

Verse 18 — *I should be growing in* _____
_____

"How can I repay the LORD for all his goodness to me? I will lift up the cup of salvation and call on the name of the LORD."
—Psalms 116:12-13

FOUNDATION TRUTH: As redeemed sinners, our only reasonable response to the goodness and mercy of God is absolute surrender.

Go back through Lesson Seven and review the seven **Foundation Truths** that you learned. Rewrite these truths below.

1) _____
_____

2) _____
_____

3) _____
_____
_____

4) _____
_____
_____
_____

5) _____
_____
_____

6) _____
_____
_____
_____

7) _____
_____
_____

GLOSSARY OF BIBLICAL WORDS AND TERMS

ABIDE — *"To stay, remain, to continue in a place, to endure without yielding."*

In order for us to have an intimate relationship with Jesus Christ and a victorious life we must remain close to Him, talking to Him in prayer and hearing Him speak to us through His Word.

See Psalms 91:1 and John 15:4-10.

ACCOUNTABILITY — *"Subject to giving an account, answerable, a statement explaining one's conduct."*

As members of the body of Christ God calls us to accountability with one another for the purpose of encouragement, protection, exhortation and correction.

See Luke 9:10, Romans 14:12, Galatians 6:1 and 1 Peter 4:5.

ADOPTION — *"To choose, to embrace, to take as one's own what is another's."*

When a sinner repents and receives Christ as Savior and Lord he is adopted, taken into God's family and becomes a child of God. He then possesses all family rights, including access to the Father and a sharing in the divine inheritance. The indwelling Holy Spirit confirms in his heart that he is a child of God.

See Hosea 1:10, John 20:17 and Romans 8:14,15,17.

APOSTLE — *"A messenger; one sent out on a mission who derives his authority from the sender."*

Jesus Christ called the twelve disciples to Himself, then send them out into the world to do His will and fulfill His plan.

See Matthew 28:18-20, Romans 1:1 and Galatians 1:1.

BORN AGAIN — *"Spiritual rebirth."*

Every human experiences *physical* birth. When sinners repent and accept Jesus Christ as Lord and Savior they are born again by the Holy Spirit. God's Spirit comes to live in their heart, imparting to them the very life of God.

See Ezekiel 36:26,27 and John 3:1-8.

CONDEMNATION — *"To be pronounced guilty or deserving punishment."*

By nature, every human is born into sin, guilty of transgression and deserving God's

GLOSSARY

punishment. Jesus Christ took upon Himself the sin of the world and carried each man's guilt to the cross, thus pronouncing all believers innocent and justified.

See Romans 5:16-18, Romans 8:1 and Romans 13:2.

CONFESSION — *"To admit or acknowledge sin and verbally agree with God."*

When the believer is convicted by the Word of God or by the Holy Spirit that his thinking, motives, attitudes or actions are not pleasing to God and is therefore sin, the right response is confession. Genuine confession will be followed by repentance.

See 2 Samuel 12:13, and 1 John 1:9, 10.

CONVICTION — *"The state of being convinced of error or compelled to admit the truth; a strong persuasion or belief."*

Man's conscience will convict him of wrong, but only the Holy Spirit can produce conviction of sin in the heart. Conviction by the Holy Spirit urges the humble believer to confession and repentance.

See Psalm 32:3-5 and John 16:7, 8.

DISCIPLINE — *"To teach, train or instruct, training intended to elicit a specified pattern of behavior or character, includes chastening and correction, to educate, or punish."*

Because no person is born with Christian maturity and character traits, the Lord has a process of discipline in each believer's life to teach and train them in righteousness and bring them to spiritual maturity.

See Psalms 86:11 and Hebrews 12:5-11.

EDIFICATION — *"The act of building a structure. To instruct, improve or spiritually build up another believer."*

Jesus Christ came to earth to bring man into a relationship with His Father. He calls all believers to live and behave in such a way as to building up and encouraging one another spiritually.

See Romans 15:2, 1 Corinthians 14:12,26 and Ephesians 4:29.

FELLOWSHIP — *"Sharing, companionship and company; friendly relationship; a union of peers or friends."*

True Christian fellowship is both giving to and receiving from one another, focusing on Jesus Christ and the common unity of sharing and participation in His body (the church). Fellowship among believers is a result of intimate fellowship with the Savior.

See John 17:3, 21, 1 Corinthians 1:9 and 1 John 1:3-7.

GLOSSARY

GLORIFY — *"To bestow honor, praise, or admiration, to esteem; to shed splendor on."*

The believer's life glorifies God when he turns from unrighteousness and lives in submission to God's will, in obedience to God's Word and in love with the Savior.

See Matthew 5:16, 1 Corinthians 6:20, and Revelation 15:4.

GRACE — *"God's unearned favor and love."*

Grace is the goodness of God to the undeserving; the forgiveness of sins granted entirely out of His kindness, completely apart from any merit on the part of the person forgiven.

See Lamentations 3:22, Romans 5:1,2 and Romans 6:14,15.

HUMILITY — *"Not proud, haughty; arrogant or assertive; lowly; reflecting a spirit of submission."*

Humility is the opposite of pride. As an attribute of God's character, humility is demonstrated in that while God is high and great, yet He lowers Himself to be concerned with man, whom He created. God pours forth His grace upon the humble.

See Psalms 113:5,6 and James 4:6.

INTIMATE — *"Marked by very close association, contact or familiarity. Warm friendship developing through long association. Suggesting informal warmth or privacy; of a very personal or private nature."*

Jesus Christ did not died on the cross in order to form the Christian religion, but to make a way for fallen man to be made right with God and share in an intimate relationship with Him.

See Proverbs 3:32 and John 15:15.

JUSTIFICATION OR JUSTIFY — *"To declare just and righteous, to pardon and absolve from guilt and punishment."*

A verdict or judgement rendered by a judge in a courtroom. Justification is the opposite of condemnation. As man's judge God will render to each a verdict of justified or condemned. God's children are pardoned, or justified in Christ.

See Isaiah 53:11 and Romans 3:28.

MERCY — *"The outward manifestation of pity. It assumes need on the part of him who receives it, and resources adequate to meet the need on the part of him who shows it."*

Mercy is an attribute of God, who is rich in mercy, kindness or good will toward the miserable and afflicted and joined with a desire to help them. Though all mankind is guilty before God, having transgressed His commands, He extends mercy, rather than judgement to all who receive Christ as Savior and Lord.

See Exodus 34:6 and Ephesians 2:4.

GLOSSARY

PRIDE — *"Refusing to depend on and submit to God; putting faith or trust in one's self and one's own abilities."*

Pride is the opposite of humility. Pride is self-righteousness, self-seeking, self-reliance and independence from God. God resists the proud.

See Proverbs 11:2, 16:18, Isaiah 2:17 and 1 John 2:16, James 4:6.

PROPITIATION — *"To gain or regain the favor or good will of, to appease, conciliate, atone or satisfy. "*

Because God is holy and vehemently opposed to evil, He will judge sinful mankind. The *wrath of God* is His just and holy anger directed at man's sin. When Jesus Christ gave His life on the cross, He took upon Himself all of the sin and unrighteousness of man. His blood sacrifice satisfied the wrath of God. Jesus is the propitiation for our sins. All who confess their sin to God and accept Christ as Savior and Lord are forgiven and receive God's grace rather than His wrath.

See Psalms 7:11-13 and 1 John 2:1,2.

RECONCILIATION — *"To restore to friendship or harmony."*

God's Word clearly teaches that sinners are enemies of God, deserving His wrath. Christ died to put away man's sin. By dealing with the enmity between man and God, Jesus has made it possible for man to be reconciled to God.

See Romans 5:10 and 2 Corinthians 5:18, 19.

REDEMPTION OR REDEEM — *"To buy back again, to recover by payment, to ransom, or to liberate."*

In the Garden of Eden man turned from the living God and yielded to Satan, thus becoming Satan's servant. In this fallen state man was no longer free to choose, but enslaved to God's enemy. Jesus Christ redeemed or ransomed man back to God through His death and resurrection. Believers are liberated in Christ, while non-believers continue to be held in slavery to Satan.

See Mark 10:45 and 1 Peter 1:18, 19.

REPENTANCE — *"To turn from sin and dedicate oneself to God; to feel regret; to change one's mind; to feel sorrow."*

Repentance must follow confession of sin. When the believer truly regrets and is sorry for his sin, he will turn from that sin, dedicate himself to God and walk in God's grace.

See Matthew 3:8, Acts 26:20b and Ephesians 4:28.

RIGHTEOUS — *"Innocent, conformity to law, to be absolved or acquitted from guilt."*

According to Scripture, the righteous are those who walk with God in contrast to the evil who do not walk with God. Fallen sinners are only made righteous through the righteousness imparted to them by Jesus Christ upon salvation.

See Genesis 6:9, Romans 5:19.

SANCTIFICATION — *"To dedicate. Separation or setting apart of the sacred from the sinful to make it holy."*

Sanctification has three aspects, initial, progressive, and ultimate. God sanctifies the believer at the moment of salvation. He continues or progresses in the sanctification process as the believer walks with Him in fellowship and obedience. Ultimate, complete sanctification will occur the when the believer meets the Savior in eternity.

See 1 Corinthians 6:11, 1 Thessalonians 5:23 and 1 John 3:2.

SIN — *"Transgression against God."*

Sin is any offense against or violation of God's Word, authority, goodness, wisdom, justice or grace. Sin proceeds from a rebellious heart or a deceived mind and is acted upon with attitudes, thoughts, words or actions.

See Psalms 51:4, 1 John 3:4 and Romans 14:23.

SOVEREIGN — *"Over or above, possessed of supreme power and ultimate authority. A ruler."*

God, being sovereign possesses supreme power, unlimited wisdom and absolute authority. There is not a person or thing that is not under His control and foreknown plan.

See Psalms 139:1-16, Daniel 4:35 and Revelation 4:11.

TRANSFORM — *"To change a thing into another or from one form to another, metamorphose."* As we walk in an intimate relationship with Jesus Christ, He works in us to transform our lives to reflect His image and character. When we enter eternity we will be completely transformed to reflect His glory.

See 1 Corinthians 15:51,52, 2 Corinthians 3:18, Philippians 3:21, 1 John 3:2

TRANSGRESSION OR TRANSGRESSOR — *"To pass beyond a boundary, to violate or break a law or command."*

God established His standard of righteousness in the Ten Commandments. From the beginning man transgressed God's laws , and became a transgressor. Jesus Christ came to earth to fulfill the Law, to bare man's sin on the cross and secure justification to all who would believe in Him.

See Isaiah 53:12, Matthew 5:17, Romans 5:18, 7:12 and Hebrews 2:2.

THANKS FOR JOINING US!

Dear Disciple,

I pray that this study has blessed you and encouraged you to develop a closer walk with the Lord. It is important to know these fundamental truths and doctrines of the faith, and equally important for you to make a commitment to establish daily fellowship with Jesus Christ. As we abide in Him each day we experience His blessings, our minds are renewed with His truth, we are able to maintain an eternal perspective and we are filled with His grace and strength to live victorious lives. I exhort you to maintain daily devotion with the Lord, spending time with Him in prayer, reading His Word and meditating upon the things he speaks to you.

Finally, I want to encourage you to disciple someone else, taking him or her through this discipleship study. As a husband, it may be your wife; as a parent, your own children; or choose another family member, a friend or a co-worker. Seek the Lord and He will guide you in this.

May the Lord bless you and keep you.

Your brother in Christ,

Pastor Craig Caster

HOW TO DEVELOP INTIMACY WITH GOD THROUGH DAILY DEVOTIONS

Intimacy — *Marked by a very close association, contact or friendship developing through long association; very familiar; suggesting informal warmth or privacy; of a very personal nature.*

1. **SET A TIME.** Choose the best time of day (morning or evening) to commit to setting aside devotional time. Don't set yourself up for discouragement by setting a goal that you will not be able to keep. Start small, and then add time as you grow. Begin with 15 minutes.

2. **CHOOSE A BOOK OF THE BIBLE.** Read one chapter, or less if it is a long chapter or verses that you want to ponder. In addition, you may also want to read a daily devotional. See suggestions listed below.

3. **PRAY.** Specifically pray over the truths you have read, asking God to speak to you about how you can obey; what you should do or what you should change in your life in order to obey.

4. **LISTEN.** Spend a few minutes in quiet listening. This may be uncomfortable for you at first. Living in a noise-filled world, most of us are not accustomed to sitting quietly. Persevere and God will be faithful to speak to you. Remember that the Holy Spirit is dwelling in your heart and mind and can minister to you in your thoughts!

5. **JOURNAL.** Write out what these verses mean to you, and record what the Lord speaks to your heart.

    Journal — *A record of experiences, ideas or reflections kept regularly for private use.*

6. **PRAY AGAIN.** Pray using the following "ACTS" method to help you pray effectively:

    A   **ADORATION** — Worship and praise God
    C   **CONFESSION** — Confess and repent of any known sins
    T   **THANKSGIVING** — Expressing gratitude for God's blessings in your life
    S   **SUPPLICATION** — Humbly make requests for your needs and the needs of others

    Then pray that God will help you to know and acknowledge His presence throughout your day.

SUGGESTED DEVOTIONALS:

My Utmost for His Highest, by Oswald Chambers
Streams in the Desert, by Mrs. Charles E. Cowman
The One Year Book of Psalms, by William J Petersen and Randy Petersen
Meet the Bible, by Philip Yancey and Brenda Quinn
Everyday With Jesus, by Greg Laurie
Drawing Near, by John F. MacArthur
Planters Perspective, Through-the-Bible Devotionals, by Rick Lancaster

BIBLICAL PRINCIPLES FOR A STRONG FOUNDATION

FOUR DISTINCT DESIGNS, ONE FABULOUS DEVOTIONAL!

IT'S THE SAME GREAT DEVOTIONAL, BUT DESIGNED JUST FOR YOU!

With four separate designs, each version has the same content, page for page, so you can use them interchangeably — in any combination — in your group study. Just pick one that suits you best!

This devotional will help you develop a daily devotional time, to set aside time to hear from God through His Word (the bible), and to teach you about your faith — the important doctrines and beliefs of Christianity, and God's wonderful promises to us as His children.

This workbook covers such topics as: How to have Intimacy with Christ, Spiritual Growth and Maturity, Forgiveness and Reconciliation, Spiritual Warfare, and Our Eternal Destiny.

Designed for personal, one-on-one, or small group study. Designed for you!

BIBLICAL PRINCIPLES FOR A STRONG FOUNDATION
108 pages, BW, Perfect Bound, $8

ISBN# 1-60039-174-5 — Men *ISBN# 1-60039-175-3 — Young Men*
ISBN# 1-60039-176-1 — Women *ISBN# 1-60039-177-X — Young Women*

ORDER NOW AT WWW.LAMPPOSTBOOKSTORE.COM